'One of the most overlooked areas
complex dance between autism, ge
Lawson's tender, frank and beautifu..., observed account of
the evolution of his relationship to himself and his beloved
Beatrice deals honestly with the complexities of these issues,
while also being a touching and deeply human love story.
"There are more forms of gender," Lawson writes, "than stars
in the sky." *Transitioning Together* is a brave and pioneering map
of this still-unexplored terrain.'

– Steve Silberman, author of NeuroTribes:
The Legacy of Autism and How to Think Smarter
About People Who Think Differently

'Books by Wenn have always explored the frontiers of autism.
This is the love story of Wenn and Beatrice that, through the
years, became an exploration of gender and identity. I now see
an increasing number of clients who are travelling the same
road and this will be their travel guide.'

– Tony Attwood, Minds and Hearts Clinic, Brisbane

'A wonderful multifaceted account of discovering sexuality,
exploring gender identity and living with autism, wrapped up
in a beautifully honest and inspiring love story of one couple's
journey of overcoming obstacles to find each other, to find
themselves and to find a way to move forward together. It is
impossible not to feel completely privileged to be able to share
in their unique experience of undergoing gender transition
as a couple.'

*– Finlay Games (finntheinfinncible), transgender
advocate and educator, and YouTube host and blogger
on gender transition, mental health and recovery*

'*Transitioning Together* is a love story with a twist. Or rather two twists. It is the story of Beatrice and Wenn overcoming personal battles to come together as a lesbian couple in the mid-80s, at a time when such things were very frowned upon, and it is the story of the same couple coping when, decades later, Wenn realises that he is transgender – a trans man. Touching and insightful, as trans comes "out of the closet", this is an increasingly relevant story for our times, as individuals must come to terms with how this, too, impacts upon their relationship.'

– Jane Fae, journalist and campaigner

Transitioning Together

by the same author

Older Adults and Autism Spectrum Conditions
An Introduction and Guide
Wenn Lawson
Foreword by Carol Povey
ISBN 978 1 84905 961 9
eISBN 978 0 85700 813 8

Sex, Sexuality and the Autism Spectrum
Wendy Lawson
ISBN 978 1 84310 284 7
eISBN 978 1 84642 112 9

Understanding and Working with the Spectrum of Autism
An Insider's View
Wendy Lawson
ISBN 978 1 85302 971 4
eISBN 978 1 84642 229 4

Build Your Own Life
A Self-Help Guide For Individuals With Asperger Syndrome
Wendy Lawson
ISBN 978 1 84310 114 7
eISBN 978 1 84642 386 4

of related interest

Can I tell you about Gender Diversity?
A Guide for Friends, Family and Professionals
CJ Atkinson
ISBN 978 1 78592 105 6
eISBN 978 1 78450 367 3

Transitioning Together

One Couple's Journey of
Gender and Identity Discovery

Wenn B. Lawson & Beatrice M. Lawson

Jessica Kingsley *Publishers*
London and Philadelphia

First published in 2017
by Jessica Kingsley Publishers
73 Collier Street
London N1 9BE, UK
and
400 Market Street, Suite 400
Philadelphia, PA 19106, USA

www.jkp.com

Front cover image source: James Mepham
www.jamesmepham.com

Library of Congress Cataloging in Publication Data
Title: Transitioning together : one couple's journey of gender and identity
    discovery / Wenn B. Lawson and Beatrice M. Lawson.
Description: London ; Philadelphia : Jessica Kingsley Publishers, 2017. |
    Includes bibliographical references.
Identifiers: LCCN 2016038905 | ISBN 9781785921032 (alk. paper)
Subjects: LCSH: Lawson, Wenn, 1952- | Lawson, Beatrice M. | Transgender
    people--Biography | Transgender people--Identity. | Transgender
    people--Family relationships. | Female-to-male transsexuals--Biography.
Classification: LCC HQ77.8.L39 A3 2017 | DDC 306.76/8--dc23
LC record available at https://lccn.loc.gov/2016038905

British Library Cataloguing in Publication Data
A CIP catalog record for this book is available from the British Library

ISBN 978 1 78592 103 2
eISBN 978 1 78450 365 9

Printed and bound in the United States

Publisher's Note

When Wenn, Beatrice and I first discussed this book, we agreed that the feelings and responses Beatrice generously felt able to share about her journey through Wenn's transition were enormously valuable and important, validating the experiences of many others. In staying true to the story as it unfolded, we felt it important to use gendered pronouns reflecting Beatrice's experience at the time, rather than the reality of Wenn's essential male identity. I hope readers will understand and accommodate the reason for this unusual usage.

Jessica Kingsley

Contents

Acknowledgements

To my gorgeous, loving and courageous wife, without whom this story couldn't have been written, I owe a debt more than words can describe. It's because of you and your commitment to uncovering our truth, to facing the demons that have haunted you, to choosing life and daily surrender to what that brings, that our journey together continues.

We have so many amazing and wonderful friends who have supported us throughout the journey mapped out in the story within the pages of this book. Some, in particular, despite the difficulties and hurdles our chosen lifestyle presented to them, never wavered in their unconditional love and acceptance of who we were:

To Dr Dinah Murray we owe a true debt of friendship that sincerely pays out in kind; Dinah, not only for proofreading our work, but for accepting and supporting us in countless ways over the last 18 years, thank you.

Suzette, you have always been not only a supportive friend to both Beatrice and I but that person we could come to with anything that bothered us. Your prayers, hugs and tears, along with ours, are dyed into the very fabric of our being and helped paint the path to self-acceptance we are enjoying today.

To each of our children and grandchildren, we say thank you. Being part of an inclusive family gives us each a home. Knowing we have a place in your hearts, just the way we are, inspires us to keep on keeping on!

Paul M., you are always there when we need you. The parallels our lives have shared never cease to amaze me. From Exodus days to you telling me: 'I always knew you were trans and I was waiting for the day you knew it too!' Your ability to accept and work with what comes your way stands you in good stead for the future you are building, here today. Love your garden, dear friend!

Maryanne, thank you for all those cups of coffee and long chats at whatever time of day! You gave us time, but you also gave us yourself and the will to keep fighting. So many times we might have given up...meeting and having a friend whose heart is one with ours, who truly 'gets' who we are, is magic. For all your feedback on this book, the wisdom and guidance, dear friend, thank you!

Paul J. – the journeys in your car and so many times of having us in your home; those impromptu lessons and advice on understanding women; the etiquette on male issues and having the right hair cut – you just know how to affirm me. Both Beatrice and I value your love and acceptance. Thank you.

Janet, your walks and talks supported our journey towards understanding the bigger picture. You are a great listener; your wisdom, acceptance of the pain that loving another can bring, shared hope and friendship mean so much.

Thank you to fellow trans guys who have shared the ups and downs of their journeys with us and offered the knowledge and experiences from their perspectives – totally invaluable!

Jimmy, Matthias, Finn, Dade and all those others we read of or watched over the Internet, thank you.

To the doctors and teams of medical staff around the globe committed to making the lives of trans individuals less dysphoric and more whole – it's thanks to you we hold our heads up high and can take up our place in the world again. One day though, it will be easier.

Thank you to all of our friends and adopted family around the world whose love and support holds us during trying times and who celebrate with us the precious life-giving moments we cherish: the Browns; Bruce and Carolyn; Brynn; the Clarks; the CRC team; Dave and Flave; George and Mal; Glen and Lainie; the Greens; Jessica; Katy Harris; Lee; Rita, Zaff and Lucy; Susan; the Talbots (my wonderful Tassie and Isle of Wight family); and Vicki. Plus all those others who have dipped into our lives at various times; you know who you are!

This book is the most important book I have contributed to, to date. It celebrates all that is good and precious amongst the treasure that is human nature. It challenges the junk and baggage of ill-informed bigotry and, most of all, it blows away the chaff to help surface and shine the gold of who we each are. Thank you!

Preface

This story is about two people who love and care for each other very much. These two individuals – born almost 12 years apart in different countries with different cultures – were both assigned 'female' at birth. In many ways they had lots of things in common; for example, they were both born into a family where they were one of four offspring. Both sets of parents had experienced living through the Second World War, or post-war years, and knew what it was to be hungry, in poverty and then grow into richer years and be governed by ambition for their children.

The younger individual came from a Swiss mountain village, in the German-speaking part of Switzerland, an hour southeast of Zurich. Her father was a practical man in some ways, but he didn't have a head for figures. He loved the forest and spent much time collecting firewood, ran a thriving butchers shop in the local village, kept rabbits, chickens and at times sheep, and in retirement sometimes helped his son as a lay person, to assist with arrangements and matters in their local Catholic Church.

The older individual was from England and had travelled around that country living in several different counties.

Like the father of the younger individual, but more so, this older individual's father was also practical. He tinkered with engines, built and invented things, was a bit of a dreamer who loved to sing and play the squeeze box and worked at various things including being a fireman, restaurant manager and chef, publican and security guard. He also didn't have a head for figures.

Because they did have a head for figures, both wives of these men were more the business managers for their husbands' businesses and families. The younger individual's mother loved to sing, was very social and outgoing and worked hard alongside her husband in their shop. This resulted in the younger individual in this story being left to her own devices whilst her parents worked in the shop. Consequently she developed a core belief system where she would often be abandoned or not important enough to be included. This belief system saw many of her actions, as an older person, born from fear of rejection, beliefs of unimportance and the need to control to protect herself from being abandoned. This individual found social situations very painful and avoided them as much as possible. It should be noted that the contributions to this book from the younger individual are all the more important to treasure because it is so uncomfortable and difficult for her to expose her inner thoughts and feelings so publicly.

The older individual in this story was the eldest of three daughters and born nine years after her brother. This brother didn't emotionally connect to his father who was away during the first three years of his son's life, a soldier fighting for his country. Father and son never really bonded.

The older individual's mother was not a social person and, although she supported her husband in all of his ventures, it was always a chore to mix with other people. Unlike her husband she was tone deaf and music was noise that irritated rather than something to be enjoyed. Although the older individual in this story was somewhat of an enigma to her father, they shared much together. They both loved engines, music and singing, creativity, spontaneity and sharing stories together with other people.

We are often told that 'opposites attract'. We are also told that many partners are attracted to each other based on what is familiar to them, which is why so many of us choose a spouse who turns out to be a lot like one of our parents! The older individual in this story fell in love with a woman who was very good with figures. The younger individual in this story fell in love with a 'wo-man' who did not have a head for figures.

The following story is about a journey to uncover and pursue true gender identity and its impact upon one married couple, the older and younger individuals from the description above. At first glance it appears to paint a picture of one female discovering 'she' is a 'he'. But this story is not just about him. When the one partner, in this story, questions and then explores their gender identity it impacts upon the other partner and both realise they had been living from core beliefs and hidden identities that were incomplete or based upon foundations borne from injury, insult and injustice. This story is about both individuals discovering their real identity – of living with gender dysphoria, autism, poor mental health, disability, learning difficulties, codependency, discovery of truth, forgiveness and much more. It is about what it means to be a person growing up in an imperfect world.

The older individual (Wenn) narrates this story in roman font with the younger individual adding her words, which are in italics and are prefaced by her name, Beatrice.

This is a very important story because it is the story of being human; it's the story of *us*.

Notes on Sex and Gender

Gender

This usually refers to one's biological sex and/or identity. It is a social and cultural construct of what constitutes being a 'man' or a 'woman'. This is based on the characteristics that a society or culture perceives to be 'masculine' or 'feminine'. Of course, there are a number of 'genders' that don't fit neatly into such a box! More and more we are seeing male–female plasticity; the conclusion to date is that gender spans a continuum or spectrum, and is not a binary construct so much as a brain/perception disposition.

Biological sex

This usually refers to the male or female sex characteristics such as a penis, vagina, ovaries and testes.

Sexuality

This is a central feature of being human that is deeply individualised. It includes sexual feelings, thoughts, attractions, preferences and sometimes behaviour.

Sex in the brain

Our biggest sex organ is our brain. There is no such thing as a male or female brain, but brain differences occur in males and females. We do not have a gender-free society. Gender equality is not the same as gender free.

The following is taken from the World Health Organization.[1]

Genetic Components of Sex and Gender

Humans are usually born with 46 chromosomes in 23 pairs. The X and Y chromosomes determine a person's sex. Most women are 46XX and most men are 46XY. Research suggests, however, that in a few births per thousand some individuals will be born with a single sex chromosome (45X or 45Y) (sex monosomies) and some with three or more sex chromosomes (47XXX, 47XYY or 47XXY, etc.) (sex polysomies). In addition, some males are born 46XX due to the translocation of a tiny section of the sex determining region of the Y chromosome. Similarly some females are also born 46XY due to mutations in the Y chromosome. Clearly, there are not only females who are XX and males who are XY, but rather, there is a range of chromosome complements, hormone balances, and phenotypic variations that determine sex.

The biological differences between men and women result from two processes: sex determination and differentiation.[2] The biological process of sex determination controls whether the male or female sexual differentiation pathway will be followed. The process of biological sex differentiation (development of a given sex) involves many genetically regulated, hierarchical developmental steps. More than 95% of the Y chromosome is male-specific[3] and a single copy of the Y chromosome is able to induce testicular differentiation of the embryonic

---

1   www.who.int/genomics/gender/en/index1.html

2   Goodfellow P.N. *SRY and sex determination in mammals.* Annual Review of Genetics, 1993, 27:71–92.

3   Willard H.F. *Tales of the Y chromosome.* Nature, 2003, 423:810–813.

gonad. The Y chromosome acts as a dominant inducer of male phenotype and individuals having four X chromosomes and one Y chromosome (49XXXXY) are phenotypically male.[4] When a Y chromosome is present, early embryonic testes develop around the 10th week of pregnancy. In the absence of both a Y chromosome and the influence of a testis-determining factor (TDF), ovaries develop.

Gender, typically described in terms of masculinity and femininity, is a social construction that varies across different cultures and over time.[5] There are a number of cultures, for example, in which greater gender diversity exists and sex and gender are not always neatly divided along binary lines such as male and female or homosexual and heterosexual. The Berdache in North America, the fa'afafine (Samoan for 'the way of a woman') in the Pacific, and the kathoey in Thailand are all examples of different gender categories that differ from the traditional Western division of people into males and females. Further, among certain North American native communities, gender is seen more in terms of a continuum than categories, with special acknowledgement of 'two-spirited' people who encompass both masculine and feminine qualities and characteristics. It is apparent, then, that different cultures have taken different approaches to creating gender distinctions, with more or less recognition of fluidity and complexity of gender.

Gender dysphoria

Living with gender dysphoria impacts different individuals in a variety of ways. Dysphoria with one's gender implies a state of disconnection,

---

4   Passarge E. *Colour atlas of genetics*. New York, Thieme Medical Publishers, 1995, p.324.

5   Wood J.T. *Gendered lives: communication, gender, and culture*, 2nd ed. Belmont, California, Wadsworth Publishing Company, 1997.

discomfort and dissatisfaction; a feeling of perceived 'wrongness, for that gender'. This feeling can vary in intensity and runs along a spectrum of discord, from extreme disconnection to less so.

Gender dysphoria, therefore, implies an individual assigned a particular 'gender' at birth growing up feeling little or no identification with that gender. Often, individuals will want to be referred to as someone of the gender they believe they are. This is not a psychiatric or mental condition so much as a biological one.

Some research suggests gender dislocation occurs in utero. The developing foetus does not 'show' its sex until around seven or eight weeks when the particular sex chromosome is activated. After activation the developing baby usually forms either male reproductive organs (penis, testes, gonads and so on) or female reproductive organs (ovaries, vagina, womb and so on). As the developing baby's sex organs are formed, so there is a corresponding hormone wash in the brain. Some suggest this activity, allowing body and brain sex to unitedly inform gender, can fail to synchronise, thus leaving a developing anatomical female with a masculinised brain and vice versa. This research is theoretical though and needs much more exploration.[6]

We know, however, that gender identity is a developing concept shaped very much by societal expectation and not only DNA:

> The gender identity of a fetus, and later of an infant, is still incomplete by definition. Until a self-conceptualization of such an identity can take place, it remains in flux. At the same time, current research indicates that, because of the expected hormonal exposure secondary to genetic sex, all newborns probably have a certain gender bias toward a particular gender identity. Predicting this based on external anatomy or on other

---

6   See www.sciencedaily.com/releases/2015/02/150213112317.htm and
     www.nhsinform.com/health-library/articles/g/gender-dysphoria/causes

factors is not completely accurate because no specific means exist to verify the presupposition. In a small minority of newborns, it is also possible that the gender bias is neutral, in which case it may remain so or may be modified via environmental and epigenetic (or other gene-influencing) mechanisms.[7]

The DSM-5's definition of a gender dysphoria is available online.[8] At times the feeling of dysphoria can be so intense that some little 'boys' want to cut off their penis and some 'girls' refuse to notice their breasts or accommodate menstruation. For others there will be a gradual recognition of the things they feel; not so much a total dissatisfaction with their 'assigned birth gender' but more a discomfort and movement away from any traditional association and ultimately a desire to be treated along the lines of the gender they feel more at home in. For some, their 'gender' awareness and disposition changes according to how they feel on the day (e.g. 'I'm a boy today but yesterday I was a girl').

There are more forms of gender than stars in the sky! To describe gender in binary terms is short sighted and fails to accommodate the more extensive human experience. I imagine living in a world where each person can live in harmony with themselves, whatever their gender identity. Where, if an individual is male, female, somewhere in between or neither, they are equally welcome.

Transgender

The following story is a love story about one couple discovering their true identity as one partner moves from one gender to another and the impact this has upon both partners. Transitioning, in that sense, is all about moving and about change.

---

7   From http://emedicine.medscape.com/article/917990-overview

8   See www.dsm5.org/documents/gender%20dysphoria%20fact%20sheet.pdf;
    the reference for the DSM-5 more generally is APA (American Psychiatric
    Association). *Diagnostic and statistical manual of mental disorders (5th edn)*. Arlington,
    VA, American Psychiatric Publishing, 2013.

Technically, the word 'trans' means to be across from; it does not mean there has to be a movement or a journey towards. So, transgender is the term given to a gender that is across from the cis gender, which is the gender assigned at birth. For me, being 'trans', therefore, could be considered a gender all of its own (it might be male, female, both or neither).[9]

---

9   Some web pages concerning gender dysphoria: www.news-medical.net/ health/Causes-of-Gender-Dysphoria.aspx; www.huffingtonpost.com/ 2013/06/04/gender-dysphoria-dsm-5_n_3385287.html; www.nhs.uk/ Conditions/Gender-dysphoria/Pages/Causes.aspx; www.youtube.com/ watch?v=yEXL9o8cqAw; https://plus.google.com/118279113645730324236/ posts/FKK2trDERAC

CHAPTER 1

INTRODUCTION AND BACKGROUND

David and I had met when I was 16 and he was 18. We were drawn together because he had a Matchless 500cc motorbike, which became our transport to and from the youth group meetings sometimes held in a different town. Although he found conversation painful and had a pronounced stutter, when he was helping me with the clasp on my bike helmet I thought he had kind eyes. I was away from home, attending college in another city, but during holiday time we travelled on his motorbike to various functions. Over time it became the accepted norm; we were 'boyfriend and girlfriend'. Neither of us was very good with communicating socially or verbally. In many ways we were both naïve and very trusting individuals but with very set beliefs about male and female roles. After knowing one another for four years we decided to marry; especially after the youth leader at church had said we should!

We both had learning difficulties but were trying hard to build our lives in the best way we knew. My trusting and gullible nature meant I had been bullied at school and taken advantage of by the cunningness of others. However, my expectations of other people and my own actions and beliefs were founded upon the teachings of scripture, but my dreams and inner fantasy life were often based on the various television shows depicting family life I watched as an older child, such as *Little House on the Prairie* or *The Waltons*.[1]

In later years, after being misdiagnosed with various mental health issues, I was appropriately diagnosed with autism, dyspraxia, dyslexia, dyscalculia and attention deficit disorder with hyperactivity (ADHD). Beatrice was also diagnosed with a variety of mental health ailments, but eventually with autism too. She also has auditory processing difficulties and attention deficit disorder, but without hyperactivity.

We appreciate that the territory our story ventures into is fraught with politics. The LGBTIQ (lesbian, gay, bi-sexual, transgender, intersex and queer) world is a complex one and each individual has their own experience. In some ways it even seems odd to have these terms sharing the same acronym when this mixture of sexuality preferences and gender issues represents such different things; they are not sub-groups of the same thing but are very different. Maybe they have ended up together because difference is what unites them?

Being lesbian, gay or bi-sexual describes sexual orientation and is not connected to one's gender identity. Being trans means the person has lived with gender dysphoria resulting from their cis gendered 'identity' given to them at birth or when they were children, not being the one they felt at home in. Because their gender identity is not one they identify with, they may assume the gender across from their cis gender. Some individuals will take transforming hormones and surgeries to enable them to feel complete in their transgender, others will not. An intersex person is someone born with both male and

---

1   See https://en.wikipedia.org/wiki/Little_House_on_the_Prairie_(TV_series) and
     https://en.wikipedia.org/wiki/The_Waltons

female attributes; they may choose a gender identity according to which one feels more comfortable for them. This means they may decide to keep both sets of physical attributes or they may decide to have one set removed (if the decision isn't made for them when they are young). Their sexual orientation may or may not be opposite to the apparent gender they grow up with or adopt. The term 'queer' is one adopted by many individuals who don't feel comfortable in many traditional communities; it suggests a broader acceptance of gender and sexual minorities.

As individuals born in the '50s and '60s we had both grown up in very traditional and conservative families. Our lives were also embedded in Christian ideology, Beatrice as a Catholic and myself as an evangelical Christian. I tell you this because some of the embarrassment Beatrice experienced that you will read about (for example, identifying as a gay woman) wasn't 'chosen' so much as it was a legacy of her childhood and upbringing. Although she fought against this, it was an ongoing area of difficulty.

It is not our intention to offend or upset anyone; please forgive us if we don't navigate the politics of this time appropriately. Being on the autism spectrum dictates we will have difficulties noticing and interpreting social cues, social expectations and social norms. The usual 'understandings' and 'choices' that are open to the wider neuro-typical (NT) population are not so immediately available to us, as people on the spectrum. Although this is not a book about autism per se, autism governs our identity and experiences as autistic individuals, and its place in our lives must be appreciated as our story is read.

At the time our story begins, my husband and I and our four children were living in rooms within a large country estate home that belonged to a 'well-to-do' family in Surrey, England.

Coming from a typically 'working-class' family, we had never owned property of our own but had always rented or shared with others. It was 5 January 1984.

Just after my almost two-year-old son had gone down for his afternoon nap, I was invited to have afternoon tea in the drawing room to meet the new au pair. I looked forward to this because usually the au pairs and I got along well and they were a source of fun and interest. Many came from Switzerland, the German-speaking part, and some from the French-speaking part. So, it was with some excitement that I moved down the stairs from our quarters in the big house and towards the drawing room.

The drawing room was used mostly for formal gatherings. It had plush musky rose pink, deep pile carpet and olive green velvety drapes, tied back against the flowery wallpapered walls with a flaxen plaited cord. In the middle of the formal dining section, set back away from the lounge area, was a large dining table with chairs to match, and on the towering, echoey walls there were large paintings of village life, plus two portraits of family ancestors. However, when I called into the room the family of the house wasn't there. Instead they had retreated to the living room, a much less formal room with a cosy fire burning in the grate. I was pleased we were in this room. It was smaller and more intimate with horse and hounds paintings on the wall and several family photographs. It had been a pretty ordinary day, a bit grey, not too cold, but one that was to change my life forever.

Christmas had come and gone and the two older children (then ten and eight years old) had started back to school. My older boy was at middle school, a bus ride away from our home, while our daughter was at the small local village school. It was almost three o'clock and they would be home soon. A good friend, who lived in the old gardener's cottage at the end of the driveway, was doing the local school run. My four-year-old was also taking a brief nap and I had a few spare moments for a cup of tea.

'Hello,' I said, as I was introduced to the new au pair, 'my name is Wendy and I live in the West Wing, although our bedrooms are upstairs.'

I was about to give more detail about my husband and our four children when the lady of the house interrupted me: 'Her name is Beatrice but she doesn't speak any English. She understands a bit of French, but her native language is Swiss German.'

'Ah,' I said, 'I don't do English very well, let alone French or German!' There was an awkward silence as my landlady gave a half smile and raised her eyes towards the ceiling. I thought to myself, 'Yes, I wish I could speak other languages, but I can't.'

I felt a shiver of angst with myself for being so 'working class' and only having had a secondary school education. I shook Beatrice's hand, as was the custom in her country, then sat beside her and accepted a cup of tea poured into a fine bone china cup with its matching saucer, and a piece of Victoria sponge cake on an equally elegant plate.

The next evening, as I was leaving our kitchen which was downstairs near the family 'play room', I came across Beatrice who was sitting in this room. It was called the play room because the children of the house and their nanny used this room for meals and play, whilst the adults ate separately in the dining room. Beatrice was on her own. Before her was a plate of sausage and mashed potato which she seemed to be enjoying. I smiled in her direction and she smiled back. I remember thinking what a lovely smile she had – it was warm and inviting.

Life with four children was pretty full on and I loved it. The kids and I did everything together. I couldn't drive, so we piled onto my bicycle to go places (Guy, the oldest, on the crossbar, Tim, the youngest, in a child carrier strapped to me, Mattie in the child seat behind Katy on the bicycle seat, and me, standing up to pedal and perching on the bicycle seat when I needed to), or we walked, pushing my youngest boy in a stroller. We had chickens who generously allowed us to take their eggs and we were allowed to pick fruit from the fruit trees when in season or unwanted by the house, and vegetables from the kitchen garden along the same terms.

Beatrice aged 20 years, in the play room eating
her first English sausages and mash

We didn't have a lot and, at times, it was a struggle to feed us all. I learnt to be very creative with cheap cuts of meat or using 'baby food' to mix with potatoes, turning this into pancakes that the children ate with grated cheese. I remember some of the harsh winters previously had seen me digging up frozen vegetables the house hadn't wanted, to boil up and make soup. I put food colouring into rice pudding and placed it into a glass bowl where the layers of green, red and yellow looked like coloured lights at a party. Although life for the children and I was filled with fun and laughter – we had picnics outside in all weathers, walked through local woods watching out for the bird life, made dens from broomsticks and sheets when we were inside, role played the various stories we read in books and all manner of other adventures – there was this aching place inside of me that I had no words for. This void seemed to haunt me and was one I hadn't been able to fill.

The man I married had appeared to be a good man. He couldn't read and write very well but he was a practical person who liked engines, making things from wood and fixing things. Not long after we were married though, it became obvious he had very poor self-esteem. Whenever I achieved something, suggested something or offered up an idea, he made light of it, often dismissing it quickly with various reasons why it couldn't be done. It was also difficult to get him engaged with family things. He saw the children as 'the mother's responsibility'. I remember tossing him a tea towel once and he threw it back to me with a sneer and the comment, 'I don't do women's work.'

Sometimes we didn't have enough money to pay bills or buy food, but David wouldn't seek help because he believed it wasn't right to accept 'welfare'. In later years I came to understand that he had social difficulties and it was very uncomfortable for him to speak to others. In a cinema or café he always wanted me to buy tickets or pay the bill. He didn't buy his own clothes, and making decisions was a nightmare for him. At times I felt like I nagged him a lot, just about ordinary things such as playing with his children.

He came from a family where he had five sisters and two brothers. The 'girls' did the domestic stuff and the 'boys' went to work. Although I could cook and clean, and loved engines, science fiction, music, books, painting and other 'arty' pursuits, I was easily disorganised, very forgetful, clumsy and not coherent in heavily social gatherings.

I think my own lack of confidence made me gullible to the abuse of others. I believed my husband would protect me and our children, but the reality was very different. Although for many years I excused his behaviour, I now know it was a form of abuse. He was very good at putting me down and sapping any confidence I might have had. I tried hard to do the things I believed a wife and mother should do, but without success. I couldn't please him, no matter how hard I tried. The more I tried, the more it seemed I was not able to be who he needed.

Eventually I grew numb inside and found it difficult to feel anything for him, but I didn't dare show it. It was a subtle process, one that happened bit by bit as the shell around my heart hardened. It wasn't that I utterly loved this man in the first place, although I certainly cared for him. At that time I don't think I knew what love was.

In the family growing up I'd always been the misfit, the odd one out. I didn't mind being on my own – in fact I loved doing my own thing. But it was uncomfortable being the scapegoat for other family issues. For example, if my sisters were teasing me, it was me who was blamed. We moved around from home to home. In one home I didn't have a bedroom – it was expected

I'd sleep on the sofa. I learnt quite quickly to hide my emotions and not let others get too close. I also became the person that others might need and could rely upon, rather than own any need I might have for others too.

When I was nine I discovered church – one of the large red brick buildings in Chippenham in the UK, with a tall steeple and a community hall at its side with, what seemed to me, amazing doorways and windows. As children my sisters and I were sent there to Sunday School. For me, it was the stained glass windows that were the allure. The colours were beautiful, especially when the sunlight crept through from outside and highlighted the individual blues, turquoises, purples, oranges, yellows and greens as it stroked the glass and chased the shadows away. I decided when I grew up I'd be a missionary, although I wasn't sure if I could live in Africa!

I didn't go to Africa or become a missionary but later, in my adult years, and with a family, I did base myself in church life, which was great. It became a place of acceptance. However, our children seemed a lot like me. They too were clumsy, disorganised and appeared to lack basic social skills. They said what they thought, loved to be free to express themselves and didn't seem to get what other people thought they should. On several occasions upon entering our small local village Church of England church, usually late, other members of the congregation would move from their pew to another one rather than sit next to us. In later years, once living in Australia, our two younger sons were diagnosed with learning difficulties too and the very youngest with autism. I believe our eldest son is also on the autism spectrum. I guess we were just not typical and, besides that, we were poor, living in and amongst some very wealthy households.

Beatrice (the au pair)

After Beatrice had been in residence a short time, the landlady spoke with me: 'Beatrice isn't getting up on time. You are up early with your children; would you help her to wake up?' Of course I would; it was no drama to make her a cup of tea at six o'clock in the morning when I made one for David and I. First though, I thought I needed to find a way to communicate with Beatrice and help her feel more at home in this cold, draughty English mansion. I invited her to join me for morning tea using gesture, the clock and a calendar. Beatrice smiled and nodded.

On the morning in question Beatrice arrived at my living room door just on 11 o'clock. I showed her the instant coffee jar and the tea caddy, to help determine what she wanted to drink. She pointed to the coffee. She also chose milk, but no sugar. My young son, not long awake after his morning nap, sat on his toddler commode (potty) and was happy playing, for a short time, with his Lego. However, each time I attempted conversation he interrupted me. It wasn't long before he needed more of my attention and it wasn't possible to give Beatrice my undivided attention. Sometime later I was to learn that Beatrice, although happy to be invited for a coffee, was unhappy and thought it rude to be invited and then not be the centre of attention! It had not been obvious to her that a small toddler would require his Mum's attention and this was a usual happening that did not take away from the joy of having her company; it did not make her less important because it was a shared time.

As the days went by I found myself spending more and more time helping Beatrice with her chores. This was anything from stitching up hems on the very large curtains covering the huge cathedral windows in the drawing room, to collecting and preparing vegetables in the main kitchen.

In our spare time we listened to music together, especially when the younger children were asleep and the older ones away at school. We used the words on the songs to match and translate with a German/English dictionary; this became a great way to communicate and greatly helped Beatrice's English. Somehow when words were put to music they were exaggerated and easier to pronounce. Within six months Beatrice's English was so good she spoke it with very little Swiss German accent.

I loved being with her but could sense there was a big sadness and heaviness about her. I very much wanted to understand what was happening for her and why she seemed so melancholy. Even though I took her a cup of tea each morning, it was still very hard for her to wake up and she seemed sluggish about her activities.

Being tuned into details that interested me

As an older child and young adult I had always enjoyed reading medical books, watching medical shows (e.g. *Emergency – Ward 10* and *Dr. Kildare*) and looking up medical terms in a medical dictionary. Hospital life had made sense to me as an individual who had spent months and months in and out of hospital, over several years, because of a bone disease that needed many surgeries. This meant hospital life was very familiar to me; it was more home than the houses we lived in. I had also been diagnosed with mental health issues in my late teens which saw me needing to be hospitalised, off and on, over many years for various treatments too. This love of all things medical fuelled my interest in what might be happening for Beatrice.

Beatrice's health at age 20

I began to notice small details, in connection to Beatrice's health, which worried me. Her fingernails were concave, her hair very thin and not healthy looking, she had difficulty in waking up, almost slurred her speech and she lacked motivation. I thumbed through my medical books, eventually alighting on the description of an underactive thyroid gland, Myxedema. Despite Beatrice's young age I believed she was suffering from this medical condition and arranged for her to see our local doctor.

After the appointment I was angry with the doctor who dismissed the diagnosis without consideration. I knew it only took a blood test to confirm or avert my suspicions, but he would not offer this. Instead he said he thought Beatrice was depressed and needed to see a psychiatrist. I didn't know what to do with this information, except ponder on it for a while. Later that year, when we emigrated to Australia and Beatrice came with us for a six–month holiday, the doctor there confirmed she was living with an underactive thyroid gland. For now though, I carried on with my life in the house, but with a heavy heart because I knew something was wrong. However, it wasn't just wrong for Beatrice, it was wrong for me too.

Wenn, the tomboy

Being a 'tomboy', as my father called me, was never questioned. I felt much more at home in boys' clothing, in more boyish pursuits and, unbeknown to any other person, I had always identified as 'Will' (from William, my father's middle name) in my inner, secret life.

I built my own sense of identity upon characters from television shows I watched. One of my favourites was a children's show called *Lassie*. In this show the boy wore denim dungarees or jeans and baseball shoes that laced up above his ankle. As a child I copied this and didn't wear traditional feminine clothing. Due to my physical disability as a child I also had to wear a full-length leg iron or caliper, and I had a built-up shoe that it hooked into. In my teens, because I had to wear a special pad over a tender skin graft on one leg, I was allowed to wear jeans which helped to keep the pad in place. So, I wore jeans to school, rather than a girl's school uniform. I never felt 'at home' in female attire or traditional female activities and took every opportunity to mix with the guys rather than the girls.

School for Wenn

Although I didn't do well at school, mostly because I was in and out of hospital and we didn't have the best traditional academic learning environment that offered assistance to children with a learning disability, I did attempt a career in nursing once my school years were over. For many reasons this failed; I ultimately did well academically (much to my surprise) but not so well in the practical arena. I used to visit hospital to be somewhere that felt familiar; hospital environments were places I felt at home. I was never successful in any traditional working environment, and after getting married at the age of 20, I didn't attempt to return to study or any form of long-term work until I was 38 years old, some 18 years later.

Awakening desire in Wenn

With Beatrice I began to notice an attraction and longing I'd tried so hard to deny in the past, mostly due to not understanding it. I had no concept of same sex attraction, no inkling I was attracted sexually to women. I knew I had formed over-attachments to my female friends and this had gotten me into trouble! With regard to social and emotional connections, I was a very late developer and not in touch, at that time, with the understanding I now have.

Life with my husband was difficult, not just because we seemed to have different expectations of one another but also because his subtle disregard for 'women' in general and emotional misogyny meant we cohabited in a home where I didn't feel safe, wanted or appreciated. For example, when I was unwell and needed help with our children, he often refused to support me. He felt angry that time given to me and the children took him away from his work. In later years my daughter said she had given up on expecting her father to make her feel special. Indeed, this was a sad thing to hear, and I felt guilty and responsible for bringing my children into a world where one of their parents was emotionally unavailable.

One day, on talking to the pastor at church, he said that if I met my husband's needs better it might help him to be more in tune with us as a family. I was given a book called *How to be the Wife of a Happy Husband*. With the church's support I tried very hard to increase my more female aspects. They encouraged me to have my ears pierced. I grew my hair longer and wore long dresses. But, while trying hard to build comfort into our relationship, my own personal discomfort began to increase even more.

Wenn's mental health

The discomfort of my perceived 'failure' as a woman, and the push from outside forces to become more feminine, only served to increase my anxiety and depression. During my mid-teens I had wrestled very much with suicidal thoughts and mental health issues. School and college life had been fraught with difficulty, and simply understanding social norms was a nightmare. This had culminated at age 17 in being sent to a mental health facility (after a suicide attempt) as an in-patient where I was assessed and (mis-) diagnosed with schizophrenia.

Today when I look back upon that time I can understand how such a misdiagnosis may occur. For example, schizophrenia usually 'enters' one's life around the mid- to late teens, and I was 17. My behaviour (I usually talked out loud to myself while pacing, and didn't always modulate the volume of my voice) suggested I was in a world of my own and disconnected from reality. Talking out loud I found to be a helpful way of trying to make sense of the world around and within myself. When the psychiatrist asked me certain questions, such as 'Do you hear voices?' and 'Do you see things?', I answered him literally: 'Yes, I hear voices, and yes, I see things.'

I remember thinking at the time: 'Silly man. Voices are meant to be heard and most people see things, unless they are blind!'

He interpreted my behaviour and my responses to these questions as someone who had disturbed affect with auditory and visual hallucinations. This was labelled as schizophrenia, a term often applied, in those days, to mental health discrepancies of unknown cause.

For the following 25 years this diagnosis labelled and defined me; it also meant 25 years of being in and out of mental health institutions. My current diagnosis involving autism could be seen to have some overlap in presentation to that of schizophrenia, and I appreciate how such a misdiagnosis might occur. Of course, one can only rely upon the expertise of the physician or professional conducting the assessment and hope they get it right! Autism is a very wide spectrum of differing levels of communication issues and impacts hugely upon perception of self and of others. In later years both Beatrice and I were to come to understand that many of the difficulties we faced with our perceptions and subsequent communication were based in our literal interpretations of an event or of someone's words. For example, much conversation people engage with consists of metaphor, which means people use words to say what they mean but these words may not mean what they say!

Feelings and emotions were also an enigma to me. At school and during my earlier adult life, I often became over-attached to a 'special' friend, which made life difficult to navigate if they weren't around. The confusion that dogged my life was amplified by my synesthesia, which meant I experienced 'emotions' as colours rather than as a 'feeling' state. However, this is a normal part of my life and not one that seems odd to me at all, just one that is difficult to share. For example, if I'm having a 'blue day', it's not so much about being 'down in the dumps' as much as it is about being anxious! For me the colour blue represents the feeling of anxiety and has nothing to do with depression.

Wenn's pregnancies and diagnoses

During a particularly rough time when I was hospitalised for several weeks, it was discovered I was three months pregnant with my first child; I was going on 22 years old at that time, but had no awareness I might be pregnant.

Once the children were born and my first child was over a year old, I was allowed to continue as a day patient, often having several weeks in between visits with occasionally being confined and admitted to hospital due to my having 'an episode'. Many years later (at the age of 42) this diagnosis was overturned, but at the time of meeting Beatrice (I was nearly 32 years old) my daily life, with my children, included daily trips to a Mental Health Day Centre as well as anti-psychotic medication given in the form of a monthly injection.

I didn't want Beatrice to know about these mental health issues and I was thankful her initial lack of the English language allowed us to keep our conversation light. As our friendship grew and we spent much of our time together, it became harder to keep secrets from her.

Beatrice: Yes, when I finally knew this about Wenn I was a bit shocked. This mother and wife who had befriended me seemed so together and capable. I would never have guessed there were any difficulties. The only thing that I had thought was a bit odd was the way Wenn walked and her clothes were not as feminine as I would have liked to have seen her in. Later, when we were living as a couple, I tried really hard to get Wenn to shop in the ladieswear part of the store, but I wasn't successful.

The incident with the car

During the first three months that Beatrice worked as an au pair for the family in the big house, it became increasingly obvious that she wasn't coping. One night in early March, the landlady knocked on my door because she couldn't find Beatrice. I asked other members of the household, including another young woman living in the house at that time, if they had seen her, but no one had. I was really worried.

Much later that night a very drunk Beatrice turned up. She had taken a car and driven to a nearby town to buy alcohol. I later found out that during this adventure she had found herself driving on the wrong side of the road and had narrowly avoided an accident.

I partly heaved and partly carried Beatrice up the main staircase, trying not to make too much noise. I didn't want to wake anyone up! Although I was relieved that Beatrice was OK, I was really concerned as to why she had done this.

Beatrice: This wasn't the usual way I responded to difficulties. I was so cross and upset with myself at my failure to perform. I was extremely miserable at that time. I missed the comforts I was used to at home in Switzerland and found the language and culture so difficult. I felt like such a failure, I couldn't stay on top of the work that was expected of me. It was awfully cold in that house too. I'd complained to the lady of the house that I was so cold; there wasn't any heating in my room. She eventually gave me a two-bar electric heater and told me to 'put more layers on, like I do'. She showed me how many layers of woolly jumpers she had on! I remember thinking that at least at home in Switzerland our homes were warm!

I had started smoking again, which was another failure. I began to go for more long walks; I loved it when Wenn came along too. We used to take the big pram and collect kindling for the open fire that Wenn would light in her living room. I enjoyed being with Wenn and her family more and more, but I disliked working for the house and found it increasingly difficult to continue.

Eventually, over time, the brewing discontent I lived with became too strong to ignore. The friendship with Beatrice opened a door to my heart and I knew I was about to succumb to feelings that were bigger than me. But I fought so hard not to, and it was almost out of anger and frustration that I finally gave in.

It was one evening in early May; Beatrice and I had gone to visit my father and stepmother for the weekend. Because I didn't drive (by then we knew we would be moving to Australia later in May), she drove me to visit them plus some other close relatives, to say goodbye. At that time my father lived in Lydd, not far from Folkstone in Kent, UK. Beatrice was having a time of feeling more connected to life and also very connected to me.

I remember us running in the field amongst the sheep and playing leapfrog as we jumped over one another. We laughed loads and it was so lovely to be silly together. That evening Beatrice tried to kiss me and I tried to fight her off. But she wouldn't take no for an answer. I was physically stronger than her, although I was older, and could usually beat her at the game of hand wrestling. In my frustration at not having her listen to me I turned her over and was on top of her, and looking into those eyes, I lowered my body until it melted into hers and I kissed her back. Making love to her, even though it started out from feelings of frustration, felt like all my Christmases had come at once! To feel so completed by another person and so fulfilled was nothing like I had ever experienced before.

The following story continues to unfold today. It gives a glimpse into an ongoing saga that still has chapters unwritten. It is a story that many might identify with. I don't know what the future holds; I do know our lives are held together tentatively by time and circumstances that we may have little say in. It's what we do with this that counts.

CHAPTER 2

A GROWING ATTRACTION

The big house where Beatrice and I met

Just over three months after Beatrice had come to live in the big pre-Victorian house, it became obvious that her unhappiness and difficulties to cope with the daily demands placed upon her were overwhelming.

The lady of the house spoke to me and voiced her concerns: 'I can't have a girl who doesn't want to be here,' she said. 'I'm worried she will do something silly. It's best she goes home to her parents.'

It turned out they were worried Beatrice might attempt suicide or some other form of self-harm. When I spoke to Beatrice about this she was very clear she couldn't go home.

The reasons for her not returning home were complicated. But, once before, when she was younger (15 years old), she had gone to the French part of Switzerland intending to stay there for a year as the au pair to a Swiss French 'well-to-do' family and to learn French. Although it was tough, she did manage to stay with them for about four months.

Eventually, though, after the summer holiday had ended, the family (who didn't really click with Beatrice) said they didn't need her any more. This was after Beatrice had much difficulty doing the things asked of her and on one occasion had ended up in tears begging her parents to let her come home. So she just couldn't do this a second time with the English au pair work. In my naivety, I suggested she come and live with us. We couldn't pay her any money but we could have her join the family and save face with her parents and family back in Switzerland.

Take a chance

During this time, Beatrice and I paid a visit to London. I had some friends there who were happy to have us to visit. In the evening on the Friday after getting a train from Dorking station to London, we went out to the cinema. Olivia Newton-John and John Travolta were starring in a movie called *Two of a Kind*. The movie wasn't one of their most successful but it spoke directly to my heart.[1]

Many of the lyrics from the movie's songs seemed to strike a chord: 'Take a chance, take a chance on love...' and 'Second time around...have it all if we only dare. When it feels so right and I'm safe and warm inside...'

The words sailed round and round inside my head. That night, with my heart beating wildly inside my chest, I really wanted to give Beatrice a kiss goodnight.

Beatrice: Yeah, it was really uncomfortable... I didn't understand what was happening with Wenn; eventually I gave her a hug and tried to go to sleep.

As the days went by Beatrice and I spent all our spare time together. Having her as part of our family seemed so right. One night in late April I instinctively kissed her goodnight. I kissed her lips, and it was as natural for me to do this as it was for a sparrow to fly.

Beatrice: I remember that kiss! It awakened an ache in me that left me wanting so much more. I'll never forget that night. I was really disappointed that Wenn didn't give me more. I wanted so much more of her than just one kiss.

The beginning of a deeper intimacy

It was after a trip to Guildford, Surrey; we had been to see Guildford Cathedral with its modern architecture and golden angel who stands tall on the cathedral roof. Being in plain

---

1   See https://en.wikipedia.org/wiki/Two_of_a_Kind_(1983_film)

view from a variety of stances across the city, I knew I needed to tell Beatrice how I felt about her, but I needed to pick my moment. Looking at the angel always gave me a sense of safety and connection. I felt less alone in his presence and, somehow, protected. I wanted to share this experience with Beatrice. We were also able to walk around some of the spring-time gardens there and enjoy a meal before we headed back.

Later that evening on the way home, we pulled into a side lane to walk and chat. I told Beatrice how I felt about her, and, without going into detail, hinted at some of my mental health issues. It was very scary. I don't think Beatrice knew what to do with the things I told her, but she smiled warmly and appeared to be responsive. She took my arm as we moved together to walk back and climb into the borrowed car to drive on towards the big house we were both imprisoned by.

A week or so later I was unwell with a cold. Beatrice came into my room to cheer me up. After some light discussion and a cup of tea, I found myself telling her of some of the childhood dramas I had experienced as a ten-year-old with my times in hospital. I'd suffered with osteomyelitis and was in hospital for almost a year. Later, during my teens, I needed a tube pedicle skin graft to cover over the tender area left after surgery to my leg. The pedicle was taken from my tummy and it had caused quite a large cavity where the skin used to be. Surgeons tried to cover it with skin from my hip, but that graft failed when the skin became infected with gas gangrene, causing the graft to die. I lifted my shirt to show her the deep pitted scars on one side of my abdomen. She dropped to her knees and kissed my battered side while crying and tenderly stroking the scarred area.

'What pain you must have felt,' she whispered gently as her tears flowed. It was such a magical moment! No one had ever commented on the pain I went through at that time or seemed to even notice it.

I cupped her chin in my open hands and kissed her tears and then her lips. I uttered one phrase only; it was all I could think of: 'Thank you,' I said.

Although we had only known each other a short time, it felt like we had shared a lifetime together and I couldn't wait to discover even more. When she showed me photographs of herself as a child in the snow surrounding the mountains near her home, or talked of her school days in the local village primary school, or of helping to gather kindling for the fire, it was as if I had been there! She was the most alive person in all of time, to me. Never before in any shade of my existence had one person touched my life so deeply.

Emigrating to Australia

Moving to Australia was the venture in progress when Beatrice first joined the house; the year before (1983) we had spent six weeks with my sister and her family in a suburb of Melbourne in Victoria, Australia. My mother, aunt, uncle and nephews lived in Australia and Mum had encouraged us to join them. 'Life is better for families here,' she had said. 'There's more work and the weather is kinder.' It was my sister who sponsored us on the grounds of a 'family re-union'.

On 15 March 1984, Beatrice went home to Switzerland and I went with her. She went to organise her visa so she could stay with us for six months when we emigrated to Australia in May. It was also a golden opportunity for me to meet her family. After the visit she then returned to stay with us and travel to Australia with us a couple of months later. The lady of the house wasn't very happy about this but she didn't object.

When my family had first visited Australia, my husband had been promised work. Upon our arrival the following year, we had a hundred dollars in our pockets, nowhere sorted to live and the promised work was nowhere in sight. So, we took up the offer to live with my sister and her family until we found alternative accommodation.

They lived in a south-east suburb of Melbourne called Mordialloc, not far from the sea. It wasn't too cold, unlike a British winter (being June, the beginning of winter in our part of Australia), and the sun shone lots during that time. Beatrice, myself and the children went out each day for walks that took us across the nearby railway lines, in and along some alleyways between the town houses and over the main road to the foreshore and beach.

Although it wasn't warm enough to go into the sea, we could walk along the sand and visit the nearby park where the children could run, swing and slide as much as they liked. They also had bar-be-ques (BBQs) there. It took a single coin to initiate the electric BBQ and we could cook sausages to add to bread and ketchup for an exciting lunch. I remember thinking: 'Wow, one could do all the cooking here and save heaps on power bills!'

Fortunately we found alternative accommodation quite soon after arriving in Australia, as living with my sister and family for two weeks was pretty uncomfortable. We were a family of seven (including Beatrice) and my sister was part of a family of four, including her two young boys, not quite two and 12 months.

As two separate families we were sharing a three-bedroomed home, with one bathroom and one kitchen. My youngest son, only two years old and not good at sleeping through the night, was still very attached to me. In order to feel safe he also needed a night light left on. The other children were also used to a night light being left on for them. But to my brother-in-law this was a waste of electricity and not necessary, so he didn't allow it. I understood we were in someone else's home and their home life operated on different rules, but I so wanted for our children to be able to feel welcome and to settle in this very different country.

My sister's smoking, these different house rules and the whole change of culture, climate and country weighed heavily upon me. None of us were used to streets, noise and so much activity.

Myself, Tim on my lap, Beatrice, Katy, Mattie and Guy, on the mulberry tree in the front garden of the big house, 1984

The children and I on a day out in August 1984; Beatrice took this picture

A stray kitten who joined our family for a while

Katy and Mattie doing gymnastics on our make-shift bed in
the main living area of our first Australian home, 1984

Beatrice with Katy and Mattie, in our first flat in Australia, 1984

Living in Australia

We had lived on twenty-eight acres of land in England. We had chickens, an apple orchard and lots of countryside to roam in. Australia had lots going for it, but it wasn't England. We couldn't wander through fields and woods (there were very few public footpaths or rights of way), even familiar foods (Cadbury chocolate, Heinz baked beans, Kellogg's cornflakes, crusty white bread) tasted different, and we had to be vigilant when it came to checking our shoes and clothing for spiders.

Whenever we went out I packed up all our needed gear into a bag and carried it on the back of the pusher (pushchair). At least we could go out and away from the house to the beach, the local shops or to a park nearby. It was this ability to be outside that helped keep us all sane.

After only two weeks of sharing with my sister's family we were fortunate; one of the local churches we had started attending had a flat that they let out. We moved in and the three boys had a bedroom, Beatrice shared a room with Katy (my daughter) and David and I slept in the living room on a mattress on the floor. This mattress was either covered in a red sheet with white polka dots (and often a great place to sleep for a stray kitten that joined us for a season)...or a blue stripy one which became a trampoline and activities area for the kids during the day!

Appropriate medical advice for Beatrice

After settling into our new home and country I found out the local medical centre would have us as new patients. Once registered for access to a doctor we made an appointment for Beatrice. The good news was that the doctor listened and conducted the appropriate tests which led to her being diagnosed with Myxedema (an underactive thyroid gland). Once she was taking thyroxine to replace the hormone she wasn't producing herself, her health and energy levels increased. However, her mood and social phobia were unchanged. She was given to depression and high anxiety which we didn't appreciate or understand at that time.

Separation

During the following six months that Beatrice was with us, the children and I developed a very strong bond with Beatrice and she with us. We richly shared our lives together, and the thought of being apart tore into our time like a bear devouring its first meal after hibernation.

That time went by very quickly and then suddenly Beatrice was gone. She was only given a six-month tourist visa and, at that time, wasn't allowed to stay permanently in Australia. That pain of separation haunted me, and my body just wasn't coping!

Owning the reality of a bad marriage and struggling with the thought of managing family life as a single mum began to dawn upon me. I knew I wasn't equipped to work or earn a living that would enable me to support our children if my husband and I divorced. The children came first, but I couldn't give Beatrice up. Instead, only four and a half months after Beatrice had joined our family (my husband and I had been married 12 years at that time), and we all had moved to Australia to try to build a different life – one where Beatrice was included – the reality hit home again.

Accounting for a short-term visa Beatrice and I knew she would have to leave, but I don't think we fully understood the agony of such a separation. Letting her go and not knowing when we would meet again was overwhelming.

Beatrice: I remember us at the airport. It was so hard saying goodbye. I had never felt such pain, it was agony. We didn't know if we would ever see one another again. I gave Wenn a silver cross necklace and she gave me a silver ring with the words 'friends forever' etched into the underside of it. We couldn't stop crying and I thought I would die. On the plane flying back to Switzerland I kept hoping no one would notice my tear-stained face or ask me if I was OK.

Over the weeks that ensued I was heartbroken. I tried really hard to reconcile my thoughts and emotions to allow myself to think beyond this woman and the way she made me feel. I kept trying to focus on my children and on church life. But all I could feel was this massive emptiness. I had to put my life into autopilot and complete tasks that needed doing, but I felt numb inside.

Beatrice and I wrote letters to each other every day and these were our lifeline. We also made tape recordings of songs, moments, thoughts and encouraging words that let each other know we were loved by the other and that love would see us through the times ahead.

My husband seemed to become more and more abusive and I found it harder and harder to respect him or be the wife he expected me to be. I went through the motions but that's where it ended. Eventually the pain in my heart seeped through into the rest of my body. My joints swelled up in my knees and made it almost unbearable to walk. Along with this physical arthritic condition and the black depression in my heart and soul, I found it really difficult to keep up the domestic duties at home.

So, I made an appointment to see the doctor. The new doctor we were registered with examined me and gave a puzzled look. He advised my husband that I needed a warmer climate and some rest. 'Either that,' he said, 'or she needs to go home to her family for a while; she seems depressed and isn't adapting to this country easily. Maybe if she goes home she will realise England isn't so far and won't feel so cut off from what's familiar.'

This all happened only weeks after Beatrice had left us. The first six months together in Australia with her beside me were difficult times, especially knowing she would have to leave us and return to Switzerland. We lived each day simply dreading the time she would go and, although it was precious to have her with me, the time was marred by the pain of knowing we would be separated, even though the full weight of what that would mean hadn't hit home.

So, with Beatrice back with her parents in Switzerland and I with the family in Australia, the toll of that separation began to show. In our exchange of letters and phone calls Beatrice was only too aware of what had been happening to me. The doctor simply confirmed this. The good thing though was it presented a golden opportunity for us to meet up again. Our being apart was inevitable, but I hadn't dared hope we could meet up again so soon!

The possibility of seeing her again gave me a reason to dream. In following the doctor's orders I knew I needed to save some money to fly to England and spend some time with family, but also with Beatrice. When I heard back from Beatrice in a letter, she said she was due some holiday time from her job and she could also take some unpaid leave. She promised she would join me for two weeks in the UK and a month in Switzerland. So, I had a mission now, to go to Europe for a holiday and meet up with my beloved. The two issues standing in my way were money for the trip and the question of who would look after the children in my absence.

Preparing for the first trip back to England

I had suffered on and off throughout my life with arthritis. The pains I experienced as a child, before formally being diagnosed, were said to be growing pains. This they may have been, but I also had juvenile arthritis and Mum knew the pain and disability this caused me. She didn't hesitate to offer to help out as best she could during this time. When I told her of the doctor's words I think she was sceptical but, even so, she and my sister said they would take care of the children while I was away.

It meant their dad taking them to the day centre and/or to school and picking them up again after work, but Mum being there to cook their tea. David had come into some unexpected money and he decided he would buy a car. This seemed like the best news because it meant the kids could get a lift to and from school or day care and didn't need to be woken up at the crack of dawn to be 'walked with the pusher'. I found out later, on my return, that the money was used elsewhere and the children, in the rain mostly, had been woken up by five a.m. and then pushed/walked to the day centre anyway. This knowledge did nothing to endear me towards my husband.

So, I had support taking care of the family in my absence, but the money for my airfares and time away was a bit harder to sort out. The children and I (as and when I was able to) went out and about to collect cans, mostly in shopping centres and sports grounds. Each squashed can was worth a cent, so we needed a hundred cans to make a dollar. It was a messy business, but Guy (my eldest son) was my hero. He collected the cans without hesitation or noticing the smell they carried, especially the beer cans. He had fun stomping on them to flatten them and make more room in our sack for further crushed, smelly cans!

Guy, sorting cans to crush, February 1985

During the first six months Beatrice had been with us I had borrowed money from her for various things. It went on shopping for groceries, school stuff and medical bills. For the first two years in Australia as a family we hadn't any kind of medical cover. At that time the 'Medicare' benefits system was being introduced but we didn't qualify. This was all very new to me. In England we had the NHS, a national health service that was open to all. It wasn't a service that individuals paid privately for but rather it was provided by tax payers and was free. Fortunately I skimped and saved and was able to pay Beatrice back this loaned money. Before she left to return to Switzerland she handed me back the loan and said, 'This is yours to use on your next trip to connect with me, whenever that is; it's not a loan but a gift.' I had never been given such a gift; $700 then was like a month's wage for some!

Beatrice: I wasn't used to giving in ways that Wenn did. My parents had taught me to save and not to spend. I wanted to see if Wenn could be trusted to keep her word. Somehow I needed to check that she wouldn't abuse it. These days I don't think that way, but back then I was young and lacked experience of true friendship.

Eventually, in March of 1985 we had collected enough cans to exchange for money and we had $800. I bought all the kids a present and said a big thank you to them for all their help. I put the earnt money with the gift from Beatrice and almost had enough for an airfare to the UK. I was on my way!

It was 30 March 1985, the morning of my leaving, and Guy, then nearly 11 years old, said to me: 'You're not coming home again are you, Mum?'

His words nearly broke my heart. All of this was so unfair on the kids! 'Of course I am,' I said. 'Nanna and Aunty Ann are going to help Daddy take care of you while I'm away. I will phone home once a week and I'll write to you too. Please don't worry.'

But Guy did worry. Over the following year he developed an ulcer and experienced much discomfort. Eventually we got him the right treatment and diet, so he recovered well. But I'll live with the guilt that as his Mummy, I contributed to his pain.

In England again!

The time away from Australia was magic and I couldn't breathe in enough of the English air, English countryside and Englishness in general. Nor could I get enough of Beatrice. I knew in my heart that we belonged together and I had to face the decision of making plans for leaving David.

This meant considering the emotional costs of divorce when you have children, and all the other things involved with property settlement and custody arrangements. It also meant sorting out the issues in my heart and head that reminded me that marriage was forever, 'for better or for worse...until death do us part'. It took a long time to admit to myself that I was an abused wife and I had lost any sense of being the person I used to be. There was also the recognition of emotional abuse (the damage caused from years of living dominated by another person) I was seeing in my children.

I felt the battle of the struggle to either remain in the situation, lose Beatrice and any hope of finding a home in her love, or leave the husband and 'take a chance on love'.

Back home in Australia and the light dawns

The few weeks away visiting family in England and the time with Beatrice whistled past and were over almost before they had begun. Were we simply delaying the inevitable? We just couldn't imagine being apart and it took every ounce of courage we had to say farewell to each other, again. How many times could we keep doing this? I couldn't think that way then, I only knew we had to find a way to be together; but the children came first. On the plane trip back to Melbourne I knew I had to explore, seriously, ways to deal with my sexuality. I adored and loved Beatrice beyond measure, but I needed to be Mum to my kids and this had to take a front seat. If I could find a way to somehow meet their needs and mine, I would do so.

After much deliberation and discussion with some trusted friends I decided to work extra hard on building support to aid and sort the confusion within me. Due to being depressed and living with so much anxiety, I sought out a counsellor at church. I was a respected church member, fully involved in church life, Sunday school and other church groups. I had tried to share my fears of not being at home in the female role, of not being attracted to my husband and men in general, of the secret suspicions that I was gay and attracted to members of my own sex. So far, trying to find someone who would listen was proving elusive.

First encounter with Exodus

The counsellor listened well, but the pastor would hear none of it! Instead they encouraged me to develop my female side. I was even made leader of a ministry that supported 'homosexuals' so they could choose not to be gay; this ministry was called Exodus. I particularly poured all my energies into this group. I came across a researcher who suggested that one could 'fill up' on same sex love (her research suggested same sex love was often lacking from the same sex parent) and could grow out of their homosexuality. To this end Beatrice and I worked hard on 'filling up' our same sex needs, without sex.

Beatrice: Well, I think Wenn worked harder than I did. I wanted her so much I didn't care that the church said we were wrong. I did feel guilty though, like I was breaking up a family. But my heart reasoned that this family was not really a whole family to start with. David was hopeless with the children, always undoing the things Wenn set in motion. He didn't command any respect from them but they constantly acted like they needed his acceptance. Small things would make him blow and you never knew what might set him off. I think I saw my role as one that rescued Wenn somewhat from this man's bullying ways. I loved the children, and it hurt so much to see them succumbing to his critical and 'put you down' ways. I couldn't wait for those times when we were on our own, without him. We built such precious memories from those times.

Exodus became very important to me, but over the following year the group dwindled and I was finding it difficult to get there. I arranged for one of the other members to share the leadership with me. Paul would collect me from home and we used to stop for doughnuts along the way! However, my involvement in leadership of this group had to ultimately stop as I came to terms with the realisation I was not growing out of my desire for Beatrice. Eventually I met a different counsellor who gave me the best advice. She said: 'When I look at you I see an individual carrying a heavy weight. It's the weight of a dead relationship. The dead relationship is like a corpse that you carry on your back which is weighing you down; it stinks and it needs a respectable funeral.' I'll never forget those words and the light they switched on for me: 'If this relationship is dead then "until death do us part" could mean I can legitimately separate from my husband. A respectable funeral could mean a divorce where the end result is no more corpse!' The hope this generated in me was massive and it fed the next few years as I built myself a stronger place to move on from.

Of course, even if David and I separated, I couldn't see a way for Beatrice and I to live together. First, she didn't have a visa that allowed her to remain in Australia, and second, I didn't have an occupation that let me earn money to support my family. I decided I needed to gain more education so I could have a chance to get work. This way more doors would be available for me to open and I would find a way for us to be together. That way did eventually open, but it was to be several years of Beatrice commuting between Australia and Switzerland before that opportunity presented itself.

Going back to school

In 1990, after we had been living in Australia for six years, I told David I would be going back to school to study the last two years of high school. I felt our youngest son was old enough now and all the children could cope. It would be an evening class course, with lessons at the weekends as well, but David would be home then and could take care of his children. He laughed at me and said the children needed their mother at home and I was too old to go to school. But, this time, I took no notice of him and I enrolled in years 11 and 12 at the local high school and dreamed of working as a writer, teacher of English or something similar that would give Beatrice and me an opportunity to explore ways to be together.

Writing and poetry had always been important to me but I was much delayed in my education. I didn't talk until I was way past my fourth birthday, and I didn't learn to read until I was nine years old. Throughout my schooling I was in a class for students who struggled academically; it was called the 'D' class. As far as the children were concerned, myself included, the D stood for dunce.

I had never thought myself very bright and I accepted my life would not amount to very much. I didn't care because I loved being Mum to my kids and I thrived on living as a family with an open home that was quick and willing to share with others in whatever way we could.

Returning to study was difficult for two main reasons. One was the practicality of academic study. This was difficult for me because reading and writing did not come easily. I also found I couldn't write notes and listen to the teacher at the same time. Second, because David resented my time being given elsewhere, he refused to care appropriately for his children. He often turned up late from work, which meant I was late getting to class. He refused to drive me to school, so I had to walk. I prepared meals for the children that just needed warming up or dishing out. Time and time again I came home to see that the food was still on the kitchen work bench where I had left it. He chose to give our children toast and jam instead.

I think he hoped I would give up and not continue with my studies. I felt bad for our children but I was only away two evenings during the week and all day at weekends. So, most evenings the children got a proper dinner and, at weekends, my mother and sister helped out, as did other friends from church. During the second year David was absent from my life and Beatrice was with me. Those two years seemed like an eternity, but eventually in 1992 I finished the exams and passed my Victorian Certificate of Education (VCE) with a high enough grade to allow me to apply for university. It was an awesome feeling! I was showing myself, my family and the world that, when motivated and interested, I could succeed.

The first undergraduate course I attended was like a dream. I drank in the times of study and sitting in the library just soaking up the information from so many amazing books. University life felt like a second skin to me. At that time I had no idea university would open up a future beyond my wildest dreams. I remember watching the movie *Educating Rita* and I identified with the main character in many ways. University life showed me an alternative view on things and it wasn't the narrow, constricted view I found in church life.

Beatrice too was working hard at finding her purpose. Her Swiss qualifications were not accepted in Australia like they were in Switzerland. So she decided to undertake a two-year college course in Australia, to gain her Associate Diploma and Advanced Certificate in Accounting. It was both exciting and difficult to navigate our studies and care for the family, but we did it. After completing her studies in 1995 we walked together to the local milk bar (corner shop) to check the newspaper for her name to see if she had succeeded in gaining entry to her chosen university course.

Beatrice: *It was an incredible moment when the local paper came out with the successful university places advertised and my name was amongst them. Wenn's daughter, Katy, had also gained a place and it was easier to find her name than it was mine. This was one reason I wasn't convinced I'd gotten in, as I couldn't find my name. Eventually we found it tucked into the crease of the paper! I got into Swimburne to do business accounting. As well as exciting though, it was very scary. I didn't expect to do very well, not because of the academic nature of the course so much as the way university studies were run. Also, I found the social side of things really difficult. Speaking and studying in a foreign language was one thing, but decoding social cues as well was another. It terrified me!*

Beatrice attempted university, but it was soon obvious that it was too overwhelming for her. The nature of the course required a lot of group work and she just wasn't able to process the expectations quickly enough. Some years later we came to understand Beatrice was living not just with autism, but also with auditory processing disorder. This meant it was very difficult to process words fast enough to keep up a conversation, and when in strange surroundings or with individuals she didn't know well, she was simply closed down by expectation. This perceived failure contributed to her times of deep depression, even though she was so uplifted by the very fact that she won a place at university to start with!

It's only on reflection as we look back at those years that we understand them so much more. Understanding our self and how we each relate to those we love – those others within our family and those we bounce our innermost thoughts off – builds a lifetime of experiences and takes a lifetime to decode.

CHAPTER 3

SEPARATION, DIVORCE,
IN-BETWEEN AND TOGETHER

*I*n the early days of our friendship Beatrice had been uncomfortable and frustrated with the situation she was moving into. She began to realise she was falling in love with me. But she thought the feelings she had were only meant for the opposite sex. She couldn't work out her feelings; she felt confused and it seemed all wrong. She kept asking herself: 'Why wasn't Wenn a man?' and 'Why do I feel this way for her?'

One day in April 1984, before we left England to travel to Australia, Beatrice had gone for a local country walk and all she could do was cry. She had been infatuated with other women in her past, but it was much more about emotional connection than it was about romantic relationships. She had boyfriends who she had admired and respected but had never allowed herself to get too close to. An older sister had to marry, as did her brother, because they expected a child. Her mother had married for the same reasons. Beatrice did not want this to happen to her, so when it came to sexual activity she kept her distance from men. If she owned the fact she was attracted to a woman it implied she was a lesbian and the whole idea appalled her.

Beatrice: It's not so much being appalled with the idea of same sex love and sex, but more that I would be an embarrassment to my family. I would have to tell them about myself, and such exposure would be overwhelmingly difficult for me. Somehow it didn't seem so bad for Wenn. Wenn didn't get embarrassed and she didn't care what people thought of her. For me, well, I would be the talk of the village! I couldn't show my face at church again. My parents would be devastated. So, yes, I was angry Wenn wasn't male, wasn't as young as me and that she wasn't single. It all made my life so complicated, and I didn't need more complications. But I loved her and couldn't bear the thought of life without her.

So I guess I buried my head in the sand and pretended we were just friends and I was an extended member of the whole family. Somehow this made it easier to cope with all those visits between countries and I didn't need to tell my parents anything about us. I showed them our holiday pictures and talked lots about the children. To them I was your 'au pair girl' and a good help to the family, nothing more.

However, as time moved on, the pretence of living as another member of our family, like an older sister to Katy and the boys, was not sustainable. Beatrice and I were inseparable. I don't know if my husband realised how important Beatrice was to me but he became increasingly difficult to live with. His emotional taunts increased and he sabotaged any project that I attempted.

For example, before going back to school to take years 11 and 12 in Australia, I discovered from an article I'd read that mature age students could attend university if they passed an entrance exam. I applied to take this exam, just to see how I would do. I certainly didn't expect to pass it. On the day of the exam I asked David to drive me to the university to take the test. I was not very good with public transport and easily became disorientated. I had attempted to pass a driving test but had failed this three times. My family concluded the roads were safer with me as a passenger only!

The university had several campus sites but I was unaware of this. David drove to one of the campus sites, knowing it was the wrong one. Our youngest son was in the back of the car. To save face in front of our son, after telling me he knew it was the wrong campus, he drove me to the right campus, especially as I insisted. He said it would be too late to take the exam, but he drove me there anyway. Once I reached the right campus the gate guard said: 'They're waiting for you in room 42b.' I couldn't believe it. The invigilator and those attending the exam were waiting for me! That exam started 20 minutes late, but I completed it in the set time and I passed. It was a magic moment that affirmed the course I was on and one I'll never forget. Although it wasn't passing that exam that gave me entry to the university course I eventually got into, it was very much part of the journey.

The more time went on, the bigger the rift became between David and I. I couldn't live with the lie any longer that we were a happily married couple. On returning from an overseas visit to England, at the end of April 1991, I told him I couldn't live with him any more and requested he look for somewhere else to live. It was a lot easier to relocate him, as one person, than for the four children and I to move out. This all seemed very logical to me. I was concerned the children were as distressed as little as possible and David agreed with this thinking. I didn't think, at that time, he would want the house or even that he might want to divvy it up 50/50. We had not long bought it, had a hefty mortgage and a deposit that had been loaned to us. So, in reality, the house was a burden and there wasn't any 'money' in it for either of us at that time.

Separation

It was 24 May 1991 that David moved into our living room, and although I still cooked for him and did his washing, we were now a separated couple. David was angry and his reactions scared me, but I knew I had to do this.

We lived like this for the following month or so and then we found David a flat, not too far away, so the children could still see him. We furnished his flat with all the bits and pieces he needed: furniture, linen, cutlery and so on. The reader may be wondering why David didn't do his own house/flat hunting. The whole idea would have been very difficult for him to navigate and would have required him to be off work to go to talk to various Real Estate agents. Although David could be very firm with me, he was not so authoritative outside the family unit.

David argued that I wouldn't last a week without him. When I close my eyes I can still hear the taunts he delivered that day.

Divorce

One year after that initial separation I applied for a 'no fault divorce'. A date for the hearing was set for 18 August 1992.

When the day arrived it felt like a huge weight was about to be lifted off my shoulders. After getting up on that morning – it was a bright sunny day, just a little cool – I dressed in my least feminine attire. I wore a purple and black satin waistcoat over a blue shirt and dark navy blue jeans that had a crease down the side of each leg. Beatrice also wore her waistcoat, but over a cream-coloured shirt and jeans. We dressed for each other and for this infamous occasion that I had once thought would never happen!

We arrived at the court at the time we had been given. Although we sat and waited while all the other morning court business happened first, we didn't mind that our case was the last one to be heard. The court room was nearly empty and I reckoned the judge was being kind to us. At first, the judge debated whether we truly met the criteria that qualified us for divorce, because I had still cooked and washed for David for those weeks before he moved out. But I assured the judge that we were not together in any marital sense of the word and that divorce was right for us.

David became quite agitated and shouted out in the court room about my dates being wrong. But Beatrice had all the dates of our times away and when David moved out; we had formal evidence by way of letters written between one another documenting this process. Rather than David's objections doing him a favour, the judge got a good glimpse of David's abusive manner; the divorce was granted.

The experience of being a single mum

For the first few months before Beatrice joined me I was a single mum. This threw up many difficult, uncomfortable and troubled moments. We had had two foster children and a couple of young people who needed lodgings join us. The foster children had moved on but we still had others in our extended family, including my mother. It was uncomfortable, for example, riding in the back of the car when being picked up to go to a parent pupil evening, rather than in the front, which in the past I had taken for granted. Then there was the demotion, not just from wife to ex-wife, but from being co-partner with my husband for so many other things. I had been the main cook, 'housewife', doer of domestic duties and so on, but, although I knew how to change a blown fuse, I'd never done it. Even though David didn't involve himself with the children unless his time was requested, he was around. However, before Beatrice joined me I had to get used to being single and doing things alone. David said I wouldn't make it without him, but I did; we did.

This happened 19 years after we were first married, but in reality our relationship had been decaying from the start. It's uncomfortable to admit this to myself, to appreciate that, although I had four beautiful children from that liaison, it was never going to be a fulfilling union. Now it was time to work out our next move, relationally, living as divorced partners with four children to care for. I had no income, no work prospects, a history of mental illness and an ex-husband who refused to pay child support towards the care of his children on the grounds he didn't earn enough.

Those times were very tough. I had a huge mortgage to pay each month and all the usual bills that families incur just from living. Throughout this time Beatrice was my rock. Although not present with me during the first few months of separation from David, by the end of December 1991 she had left Switzerland to join me as my full-time partner in Australia. This could happen for us because the Australian government had issued a particular visa allowing particular immigrants from outside Australia, if they fitted certain requirements.

The visa

In 1991, the Australian government issued a special visa called 'an interdependent visa'. This allowed individual migrants from other countries to come to Australia and stay for two years, if they shared an interdependent relationship with an Australian resident or citizen (of course, evidence was needed to support the application). Then, if they could show they lived in Australia in a mutually supportive relationship with that Australian for a further two years, with the documentation of an ongoing relationship, the interdependent visa was swapped for a residency visa. A residency visa allowed the individual to live permanently in Australia.

When I first wrote to Beatrice and told her this news I was excited beyond belief. I slipped a newspaper cutting into the letter so she could read it for herself. Not in my most hopeful dreams had it seemed possible that we would be able to live together in Australia. Now, there was a real opportunity to work together to show our relationship was valid and met the criteria for one that was interdependent. This was the opportunity we had both hoped for. If successful it meant Beatrice and I could live together as any couple might.

It was really hard waiting to receive her reply. It took a week for my letter to reach Beatrice. She then had to process what this might mean.

Although we had fantasised about being together, the actuality meant leaving her family, her country of origin, language, familiar and favourite foods, her job and all she had known. Visiting Australia many times over the previous seven years had given her a good idea of what living there might mean, but she always went back home afterwards. If she migrated to Australia this would be entirely different.

The interdependent visa, 1991

Beatrice: Yes, I knew it was what we both wanted, but the reality of it now being a possibility really hit home. How would I tell my parents? What would I tell them? They still didn't know I was a gay woman in love with another woman. They would be angry and try to talk me out of it. Wenn was almost 12 years older than me; she had four children and my parents wouldn't understand.

Sometime later, in my lounge room at home, I was watching a TV show called 'Love Boat'.[1] In the show one of the ship's crew had fallen in love with an islander and, as the boat left the island, the crew member knew he had to choose. Would he go with the ship, with all he knew, and forgo this opportunity for love? Or would he jump into the ocean and take his chances? He jumped in and swam back to the island

---

1   https://en.wikipedia.org/wiki/The_Love_Boat

to be with the woman he loved. My heart was pounding, and I just knew that this was what was required of me. I had to jump in!

I was ecstatic when I finally received the letter from Beatrice telling me she would come. It took her a couple of months to process the idea and weigh everything up. It was the longest two months ever!

Beatrice: *I was so anxious about the whole thing. I really wasn't sure if I was making the right decision. What if things didn't work out? I always tried to plan things and be organised. This was a venture that didn't allow me to see the future and I was terrified! But the scene from the show 'Love Boat' kept coming into my mind. I had to take a chance! At the end of October I handed in my notice at work.*

I had to give them two months' notice of my intention to leave. I still hadn't told my parents though and I dreaded it. Then Mum, who was epileptic, had a fall down the stairs. She lost her footing over the last few steps of the hallway staircase first thing in the morning and she hit her head badly. It was unreal. Then, whilst still recovering, she actually had another fall. Dad was taking them shopping but he moved the car before Mum was in properly so she fell and knocked her head again!

After these incidents Mum was really confused, had concussion and needed family help. Because I was the youngest and unattached, it was expected I would give the extra care she needed. But I had bought my ticket to Australia and was all set to go. I felt really guilty! When I spoke with my sister-in-law she encouraged me to go and get on with my own life. She echoed that there were enough of them to help Dad with Mum, that it would be OK. I felt terrible. It was one of the hardest things I ever had to do.

When I told my parents I was going, I couldn't give them the full picture. I bought a return ticket, as this was the expectation from Australian customs. But I let them believe I would come back after a holiday there. *On the day I left, Mum still wasn't right and she gave me a very sad look. I cried as I said my goodbyes to them at the airport.*

They didn't do hugs though, so we shook hands and gave kisses in the traditional Swiss way. It was to be nearly a year before I found the courage to write to them and tell them that Wenn and I were living as a gay couple. Mum's response was to tell me that they already knew!

Our togetherness

It was just before midnight on December 30 and, finally, there I was waiting at Melbourne Airport for Beatrice to arrive for the beginning of our lives, together. When the day that Beatrice landed in Melbourne finally arrived, a good friend drove me to the airport to meet her. During the day, by way of preparing and celebrating her arrival, I put up large coloured party lights all around the roof of our home. It was 30 December 1991. I had also booked us into a Melbourne City hotel for 31 December so we could celebrate New Year's Eve and watch 1992 arriving the next morning, together. This special time was conceived in my mind as any romantic notion might be. However, the reality was quite different!

Beatrice: *I didn't notice the coloured lights. I did feel disappointment when we went to bed because Wenn fell asleep whilst I was full of excitement. The experience of finally being here after all we had been through plus me being jet lagged meant I was wide awake. But the business of running a family and caring for three children (the eldest was away living with his father) plus preparing for my arrival had exhausted her.*

It was also very disappointing on that evening before the New Year. We had walked around Melbourne City expecting a celebration and party atmosphere. But there were no fireworks, no partying in the city streets and the city seemed mostly deserted. I was beginning to wonder if I had made the right decision! It wasn't that I was looking forward to social activity; I just had this expectation about what would usually happen at this time of year.

Meeting Beatrice at Melbourne Airport 30 December 1991

Of course I reasoned that it was just one of those things. I was tired, I didn't know where the New Year's evening celebrations might be happening and I guess I thought Beatrice would understand; at least we were together!

79

For a while after Beatrice's arrival we delayed being too open about the full explanation of her being here. We told a couple of trusted friends, who shared our excitement, and we eventually told the children. We tried to continue with church attendance, with me in a leadership role, but I guess we were very obviously in love with each other, and were told our relationship was unacceptable.

I remember telling the pastoral team that Jesus said: 'You shall know the truth and the truth shall set you free.' The 'truth', as I understood it then, was I loved Beatrice and she loved me. We wanted to be together as any couple in love might want. I couldn't deny the way I felt for her. But the church leadership didn't agree with my interpretation of that scripture and they told me if I chose to live 'in sin' it would be like putting my hand to the plough, then turning back.

It was very hard to hear these words! My Christian faith was so important to me. It was because of the love from my Heavenly Father that my life had been able to continue during the years of being married to David. Believing in the plan and love God had for us kept me going: 'I know the plans I have for you, says the lord; plans for good and not for evil. To give you the future you hope for' (Jeremiah 29:11). I now knew the future I hoped for was one that included living in a committed relationship with Beatrice.

We must be gay

The commitment to one another was the easy part, but adopting the belief 'we must be gay' did not come easily. For many, many years I had lived with an inner battle that caused so much conflict it landed me in hospital as a 17-year-old, after an attempted suicide, for psychiatric treatment. I had never felt 'comfortable' as a female. I was so much more at home in men's clothing and used to practise trying to 'pee' as a man might. Of course I wasn't very successful because I didn't have male equipment!

Once, as a 15-year-old, I had phoned a girl I really fancied to ask her out to the pictures. I disguised my voice and acted as 'manly' as I could. The girl knew who I was and was happy to play along. I was very pleased when she accepted and she didn't chide me for the pretence! But I couldn't maintain the 'act' for very long. I didn't feel like a gay woman, I felt like I should have been born male. Many years later I thought if being a butch lesbian meant I could fit into a more masculine role, then that must be who I am. I had no idea there might be other choices.

Beatrice and I tried hard to 'fit' into the gay scene but somehow it just never happened for us. We told the children we were gay and would be living as a couple. At first they seemed OK with this. Most of our friends were pretty accepting too, and we had many who were concluding that this was who they were also! But the church was not so thrilled and, now, 25 years later, nothing has changed in that department. I often miss fellowship in the way I once knew it, but I accept it's probably not going to happen.

Later, after telling the children we were 'gay', we also told my mother. Her response wasn't loving, accepting or affirming. She said: 'You were never normal!'

Mum aged 95 and her sister Joan aged 93 in our
bed at our home for Christmas, 2015

Even though she never accepted who we were, she lived in our
home from 1991 and continued to live with us for 14 years until
2005. After that time she moved into a unit that was part of a
retirement village. Today she is 96 years old and living in the
hostel part of a nursing home. Although her body is frail these
days, her mind is as sharp as a tack! She does relate more to us
than she ever did. I think she grew to appreciate our care of her,
but to this day she still doesn't accept who Beatrice and I are.

CHAPTER 4

FREEDOM

Although church had been my life for the previous two and a half decades and I was so lost outside of it, I came to discover there were blessings on the outside of church life too. Finding a renewed freedom in not having to wear 'girly clothes' and in being allowed to be more masculine was a plus. It's not that I had been told I couldn't wear my jeans and shirts to church; it was an unspoken expectation to 'dress appropriately as a female', and this meant leaving masculine attire to the casual gardening and do-it-yourself home decorating ventures, and not daily wear.

However, living as a 'butch' female gave me some licence to be a less girly female and a more masculine one.

But living as a gay couple also had many uncomfortable times where the family was concerned. Although initially the children were happy their father had moved on, they soon became unhappy that their mum was living as a lesbian. They were teased at school and their pain turned to anger towards us. Katy said: 'How could you do this to us?'

I tried to explain I wasn't 'doing this' to anyone; I was being honest and true to myself for the first time ever. It was too hard to explain to the children that coming to know yourself takes time and it took lots of courage to own the unfolding reality of a seemingly same sex sexual orientation.

So, although we had found freedom to express our love and lives with each other, it was not to the same extent as a heterosexual couple might. We didn't feel at liberty to hold hands or cuddle in public, nor around the children. Beatrice felt a sense of 'guilt' over who we were and she experienced times of deep depression and anxiety. There were also times of paranoia as Beatrice feared being exposed in general and what others might say or do to her.

Beatrice: Absolutely, I'm reminded of that time in Canada when we were walking arm in arm and those guys yelled at us – 'lesbos' was the term they used. It was so uncomfortable and you never knew if someone might actually attack you and not just call you names. Also, there were always the thoughts from the teachings of the church that said being gay was a sin and God would be very unhappy with us. I don't think I was ashamed of our love when we were together, nothing seemed more natural and right, but those old nagging beliefs and questions always dogged me.

We tried so hard to be what and who each other needed and to support the children in what they needed too. We went to see the counsellor for 'family counselling' and that was such an awful disaster. I still cringe when I think about it!

Family therapy

We thought family therapy would help support the children, and us, as we settled into our relationship together. The children loved Beatrice but they also seemed a bit lost since their Dad had left. Katy in particular almost seemed angry with us. I don't know what I expected to happen, but I didn't expect to be treated with such disrespect by the counsellor!

So, the appointment was made and we all went to the family therapy session (except Guy who was living then with his father and wasn't keen to join us). Guy was then 18, Katy 17, Mattie 13 and Tim 11. It meant travelling to the local hospital and finding the appropriate unit where such sessions were held. We took public transport to the venue and rode in a kind of forced silence which was very uncomfortable. Katy was very hostile at that time. Many years later she told me she was jealous of my relationship with Beatrice and much of her grievance then was exaggerated due to this.

The counsellor listened to the children's grievances, especially from Katy who thought it unfair that the special things I bought for Beatrice (on one occasion) and put into the fridge had Beatrice's name on. The counsellor emphasised that the children must come first, and I must choose between the children or Beatrice. She asked me who was more important to me, Beatrice or my children. I was horrified! I replied that it wasn't a case of importance. Beatrice was my lifetime partner and would be with me beyond the children leaving home. If any of the children chose to name something they were keeping in the fridge, this would be respected. I asked her if she would be saying this to us if my partner were male. She didn't answer that question. We left that session feeling very tearful and unsupported. Those memories and the associated feelings still haunt Beatrice and me today.

Family breakdown

Within the next couple of years Katy had left home to reside with a lady she knew from church. My eldest son had already left home to live with his father. This further breakdown of our family unit, with Katy's leaving, was traumatic to me and pushed me deeper into a kind of despair that was overwhelming. It had been many years since I had felt that kind of isolation, and being ostracised by the very family I had found my place with was much like being treated as a leper.

Mattie too went to live with his father and we grew further and further apart. Tragically, Mattie was killed when he was only 19 years old. He was travelling along a dual carriageway when his car hit another coming the wrong way. Mattie didn't see the car as he was overtaking another car going round a bend. Both he and the very drunk driver of the other car were killed instantly. For several weeks after that incident and all that was needed to organise Mattie's funeral, Beatrice became obsessed with the need to hover over the event. Any time we saw a car like the one that crashed into Mattie's car she had to follow it. It was her attempt to 'connect' and make sense of the senselessness of Mattie's death.

Just eight days after Mattie's death we carried his ashes in our car as we went to scatter them, with family and friends, at a nearby surf beach where he had loved to surf. We stood at the edge of the incoming tide and David took the lid off to pour the ashes into the ocean. A sudden breeze sneezed across us all and caught the dust, lifting it up and dumping it back towards us. Most of it landed on David's face and feet, missing the water entirely! Beatrice and I were sure Mattie was having one last laugh, and then he was gone. After the event a lone surfer rode the waves out in the distance and it was as if Mattie was saying goodbye. On the way there, however, Beatrice and I had a mutual, uncanny connection to Mattie. Neither of us told the other till the next day.

Beatrice: I could sense Mattie in the back seat of the car. He had his arms spread out along the top of the three-seater seat and was smiling at us. He loved that trip to the beach from home and it was one he had done often. When we got back into the car after scattering his ashes however, that sense of his presence was no more. I was unaware that Wenn had the same experience of Mattie being with us, until she told me!

A shared journey

I know it goes without saying that building a committed relationship takes time and heaps of work, but at times this needs further explanation. Beatrice and I were in this for the long haul, whatever that meant. She didn't always understand the children, but she loved them. It was interesting that many of our friends from church seemed to be on a similar journey. They too had come to a place of acceptance of who they were and had stopped fighting against their very natural same sex disposition.

The group that I once led (Exodus) eventually disbanded because its members were finding they naturally 'fell in love' with members of their own sex. Some of the opposite sex partnerships that grew from the group failed to last, and it was concluded that being attracted to members of the same sex was a biological disposition and not of one's choosing.

So, building up our family and each other in a country so far from Europe had many positives (great weather, less stress on our relationship) but many difficult times too. We both were committed Christians but were now denied the church community. We didn't seem to fit in the gay community, weren't welcome in our church community (as long as we insisted on being a couple) and couldn't relate to ordinary everyday folk.

The scripture

At times when someone from church had quoted scripture and said it was 'unnatural' to love, in a romantic way, someone of the same sex, they only deepened our wounds. The scripture said: 'We should not leave the natural for the unnatural...', but it was unnatural for me to physically 'love' the man I previously married and very natural to love the woman I was now with.

There is also some debate over the translation of the words used. For example, in Romans Chapter 1, Verse 31, the Greek word for natural love is 'astorgas'. The term for this kind of love is used elsewhere in scripture to represent 'family love' or the love for one's family. It's only 'natural' to have a special bond with your family. In general, Romans Chapter 1 talks about idolatry and false gods – about abandoning God to create other idols. The verses that are so often quoted to say that homosexual love is sinful are taken out of the context of the times. This suggests idolatry and worshipping 'things' cannot be related to loving another human being who happens to be of the same sex: 'Gay marriage honors the spirit of marriage in the Bible, honors the goal of avoiding fornication and upholds the Biblical example of accepting the cultural situation in which we find ourselves.'[1] I sometimes wonder why it's so hard for fellow humans to accept others who are different to themselves. I know it's hard to accommodate people from different cultures, but at least we can try to see things as they do.

Eventually I submitted a short story, by way of an apology, to those group members who had not only been given false hope that they could change their sexual orientation, but who had been given the message that they were not OK as they were.

---

1   See www.gaychristian101.com

The following is taken from the BeyondExGay website.[2] I was not the only person to contribute to this site, as it became the 'confessional' for other ex-Exodus leaders from around the globe.

Message to members of Exodus: As a mature adult and mother of four my Christian experience was very important to me. Not only did I attend Sunday services, I taught Sunday school; led the Wednesday evening Bible study series; and also went to Tuesday prayer meetings. Somehow keeping busy and trying to please my husband kept me from coming to terms with other evolving emotions that I hadn't time to explore or understand. Eventually, however, I could no longer hide from them.

When it became obvious to me that my 'natural desire' was not for my husband but was for a woman, I felt trapped and hopeless. I sought out any information that I could find that might be helpful. I came across an ex-gay ministry called 'Exodus'. I joined Exodus in Melbourne as a Christian wanting to change her sexual orientation. I enjoyed meeting others who were battling with the same demons as myself... somehow I didn't feel quite so alone.

After about 12 months I was nominated as leader of this small group of about 15 individuals. We met weekly for prayer, discussion and support. I traveled overseas to America to interview Elizabeth Moberley; a scholar and academic who suggested that legitimate same sex affection would provide a passage out of homosexuality. Over the next 3 years, I continued to teach, study and practice 'legitimate, non-sexual same sex affection'. However, it soon became clear to me that my homosexual drive was

2   https://beyondexgay.com/article/wendy.html

not decreasing and I was not getting any closer to becoming heterosexual.

After 4 years I decided that the truth for me was that I stop hiding and accept my homosexual self. Having assistant pastor status with my church I knew I had to tell them my decision. They felt that I could no longer continue in ministry and I was asked to step down.

Today, more than 15 years after I stepped down from leadership of the Ex-Gay ministry 'Exodus', I have come to know that nearly every member of that group is now living their lives openly as a homosexual person (20 people). I am only aware of one member who married and who would say that they are pleased not to be gay but to be living in a heterosexual relationship. They have been married for 5 years. It is also my understanding that they have not disclosed their former struggles with their partner.

Although I valued the support and friendship of the Exodus members (many are amongst my closest friends today) I suffered torment and huge anxiety all muddied by confusion and constant failure during the 'Exodus' years. For me the most traumatic outcome was my personal sense of failure as a Christian and not being accepted as a part of the church family I loved.

On April 14 2007, my long-time partner and I were married at Colchester Registry Office in the UK. This wedding celebrated who we are and our love and commitment for each other. For the first time in my adult life I felt valued for being me and thrilled to at last find a legitimate 'home' amongst my family and friends for my partner and myself.

I believe that my Heavenly Father is also pleased and relieved on our behalf. It is my sincere belief that Scripture points out that God is Love and God is Truth. The Truth shall set you free it says. Being true to my sexual orientation is freeing and I no longer struggle with anxiety, depression, confusion and sexual dysphoria!

When one is at home with one's sexual self and this causes no-one any harm and is considerate and respectful, this is love.

Beatrice and I celebrating our same sex union in 2007

The writing of the message to other Exodus members was affirming and offered a kind of release from the struggles of the time. However, the relief was short lived and didn't 'fix' the widening hole in my psyche.

Communication

Over the years that followed Beatrice and I continued to work on various relational issues. It was important to us that we were honest with one another. We learnt, over time, that neither of us was good at reading the other's mind, but it was always difficult to really believe that another human being couldn't 'read' what we were thinking. I remember thinking, 'But, if I feel it, Beatrice must do too.'

So, we simply made a pact that it didn't matter how 'silly' something seemed, we could always talk about it and that need to talk would be respected. Part of the issue though was recognising that there was an issue to talk about!

Studies and writing

After I completed my first round of studies I began writing seriously. With several attempts at getting published I finally received a favourable review of my first book. In 1998, *Life Behind Glass* was published, initially by Southern Cross University Press in New South Wales, Australia. Then, two years later, it was taken up by Jessica Kingsley Publishers, based in London, UK. When I met Jessica for lunch one day she said to me: 'This is your first book, but it won't be your last book.' Her words often echo in my mind. It's as if they give me permission to write! I'll always appreciate Jessica and her belief in me. This was not something I had enjoyed growing up and I still had lots of self-doubt.

Uncovering the person one truly is might come naturally and positively for some individuals. They might grow up in families that foster positive self-esteem, where they are welcomed in their gender identity and sexual orientation. This has to be the beginning of true freedom. Such a journey could take us places we haven't travelled before, and learning to welcome one's self beyond the family border takes even more courage!

CHAPTER 5

BUILDING CAREERS

B eatrice and I, although very different people, shared common values and have always been supportive of each other's goals and dreams. I hadn't had the education Beatrice received in that she completed her apprenticeship and was used to a working environment, while I hadn't been successful in the workplace. But now my studies opened doors for me I could never have imagined.

I also came to understand that there were reasons the children and I had such difficult times trying to fit in with regular society. Being seen as a gay woman living in a committed relationship with another woman became the excuse I used to explain so many of the difficult things that we experienced. But it didn't explain the difficulties we had with social settings or the overwhelming issues we suffered due to sensory overload.

I had worn rose-tinted glasses for several years, after stumbling upon the Irlen Foundation.[1] However, I came to recognise that these lenses helped me cope, not only with light that was too bright, but also with noisy, crowded environments. I didn't do well at university when it meant sitting in crowded,

---

1   See http://irlen.com

noisy lectures. I couldn't listen and write notes at the same time. After being diagnosed as dyslexic I was able to get support from the university in the form of a note taker and extra time during exams. This was so helpful!

In 1993 after a session with my psychiatrist in Melbourne, I suggested further assessment to explore being autistic. Initially he was sceptical.

'I'm not schizophrenic,' I said.

'Most schizophrenics don't think they are schizophrenic' was his reply!

I explained I had read a book authored by a lady who was diagnosed as autistic, but in her adult years. So much of the difficulty she lived with seemed to apply to me.

Eventually my psychiatrist wrote a referral to the team at Monash University, Melbourne, headed by Dr Lawrie Bartak. It was about six months later that I received a letter with a date for an assessment. I was 41 years old then. When that day came I travelled to the university on a bus from the highway, about 15 minutes from home. The university was like a small village and I loved the general atmosphere, but was very anxious how the assessment might go. Eventually, after another 20 minutes of trying to find the right building (the campus was a massive maze of faculties, departments, libraries and all manner of other places which included shops, bus parks and cafeterias), I came across it standing low amongst so many others. It was surrounded by a nursery school and children's play things. I walked across the courtyard and into a main reception area. There I was greeted by a receptionist and waited to be called in for the assessment.

The day with the team at Monash was amazing. It wasn't just the assessment tasks they put me through but the way they interacted with me. They took their time to explain things and were genuinely concerned for me. The small office that Dr Bartak saw me in was very plain: just a desk, chair and book shelf. There was an old computer taking over much of the desk and lots of piles of papers around it, as well as on the floor. The very well-worn leather seat I sat on seemed to contour to my shape and, despite my severe anxiety, I felt welcome.

It was one of the first times in my life I felt listened to as I tried to explain areas of concern. I'd been listened to in the past but it usually came from a perspective of mental ill health or 'what was wrong with me' and I usually ended up feeling more of a dud! But on this occasion I didn't feel that way. Part of me was expecting to be told I was emotionally wanting due to coming from a 'broken home' (my parents divorced when I was a teenager), and part of me expected to be told I needed to keep up my medication and work harder on building good self-esteem. In other words my disposition and difficulties were my own fault! But they didn't say this to me.

They said I did not have schizophrenia and I wasn't mentally ill! They said I was an individual on the autism spectrum and did not have an intellectual disability but had some learning difficulties such as dyslexia, that these were inherited or I was born this way, and it was no one's fault, just a statement of fact. I felt relieved and scared at the same time. I wasn't sure what it meant for me in terms of living my life and I didn't know what I needed to do next, except that because autism wasn't a mental illness I could challenge the need for being on medication!

When next I saw the psychiatrist I showed him the assessment (he already had his own copy) and mentioned the reasons for discontinuing with my medication. Although he was sympathetic, he thought it best not to rush into that. Although I agreed, it took a further two years before I could convince the doctor to cease my medication. I was very naïve at that time and, instead of being slowly weaned off the antipsychotic medication, I simply stopped it. I now know this was a bad idea and I'm lucky I didn't experience really bad side effects!

Life without medication took a while to settle into but I loved being more connected to my feelings and my body. Somehow the medication had caused a distance from these and, I guess, this was deemed necessary in my past. I did continue to have trouble sleeping and switching my head off from thinking and my body from feeling, but I loved how much brighter colours seemed to be and how much clearer people's voices sounded.

This newly found freedom had other implications too. It allowed me to connect deeply with the discomfort of the womanly, feminine frame I was housed in. I tried even harder to disguise this female form with more male attire and went back to shaving my lower chin and face much more frequently.

Wenn in less feminine clothes!

I also discovered that I could focus better upon my studies. The words I read became more alive and connecting than ever before. I was also able to hold on to the information I was reading so much better. I didn't have a computer to start with and writing was still quite a chore. Beatrice was so supportive in reading through my homework and essays to check for grammar and spelling mistakes. I had to complete all written work at that time by hand; there was no spell checker or grammar checker on a computer to assist me. It was tedious and laborious! So many times I felt like giving up, but I didn't. Eventually in about 1994, the university where I was studying made it compulsory for all written work to be typed and not hand written.

This was a huge ordeal for me because I didn't have a computer or typewriter. As often as I could, I used the ones in the library or at a friend's, but this was limiting because I had children and a family who needed my attention and it was difficult to be away from home at times that fitted the agenda of a library or a visit to a fellow student. So in 1994 I took out a loan with the backing of a friend and bought my first computer. It was a scary moment because computers frightened me. At that time I was a bit of a technophobe; even using a microwave was difficult for me! Almost anything that had buttons or knobs I steered away from. But despite my fears I was determined to get through my studies and master this technology.

Beatrice could touch type and had sound knowledge of Word Perfect, the software of the time that most computers operated with. She taught me how to make the most of this software: to check my spelling, delete unwanted text and move text about on the page. I never mastered touch typing with fingers from both hands but continued to type using the index finger of my right hand only. Over time though I got quite good at this and could type fast enough to get through my work. This is still the way I type today.

Although Beatrice freed me up to attend to my studies, it was a tough time for her. Her self-esteem suffered hugely through her growing-up years and she wasn't great at feeling good about herself. It didn't matter how much I said I loved her, appreciated her or how many times I exclaimed her virtues; it ran off her like water on a duck's back!

She had a father and brother who teased her. She also experienced lack of credit when it was due, was put down a lot and grew up not believing in herself. It was always that she could have done better. Her father was a man who himself had suffered through poverty and poor education. This appeared to be the foundation for his parenting. These poor role models were to have a detrimental effect upon our relationship during my transition from female to male, many years later.

For Beatrice, my success highlighted her sense of failure. It didn't take much to tip her over into negative feelings about her abilities. It was all an echo of the past. The more I succeeded in my studies and work, the worse Beatrice felt. It was as if she grieved the time these things took away from my time with her, giving her thoughts that she wasn't important. I found these times very tiring and I didn't understand what was happening for her at that time.

Today, I understand her so much more. In Beatrice's childhood she was neglected. This wasn't intentional; her parents were simply too busy to give her the time she needed and they lacked good role models for parenting. For example, her father ruled with his fists. On several occasions he physically abused the older daughters for some chore not well done, or some perceived misconduct. The brother, being the 'golden boy', was never disciplined like the girls were. In his father's eyes he could do nothing wrong. Beatrice, the youngest, mostly escaped such abuse, but unconsciously, by way of witnessing what happened to her siblings, was also a victim. She lived in fear of being hit and mistreated and was verbally abused.

Beatrice: The other thing is, Mum was very negative about men. There were moments when she said Dad was a bad person! She told many stories of her experiences of trauma and hard times with Dad. She said she could write a book about her life and could not forget the rough times with him. As well as my own experiences, her words predisposed me to fear and disrespect towards men.

For Beatrice this facilitated an ongoing need for safe attention and secure love. Unbeknown to us, we hooked each other in a number of ways that were to be challenged much later in our relationship. Although very painful to acknowledge, the transition unearthed these codependent tendencies. The good news though is that we are learning to recognise and sort them!

Beatrice: I still don't fully understand it to this day. I know I felt a strong need to find a place that I felt secure in. This meant I was driven to get Wenn to do things my way. I couldn't imagine how it might be any other way. My need to do this was born out of fear. I was so anxious that Wenn might become too independent and not need me any more. It took many, many years to admit this and to realise what I was doing. I used emotional blackmail and would withdraw affection from Wenn so she would notice me and reassure me that she loved me and I was important to her. It was a bit like a pouting child throwing a tantrum and needing her Mummy to tell her everything was OK. In some ways I allowed my fear of rejection to come into play.

In later years this changed though and Wenn did not succumb so easily. I know it's healthier to be one's own person and it's never OK to control another person, but, after the transition from female to male, I missed the 'woman' in Wenn. I think females understand each other better and are more likely to respond emotionally.

Codependency

Without realising it, Beatrice and I both had grown up with hooks allowing a codependent relationship to govern us. She needed to be 'in the centre' to feel important and I had to have someone who needed me to need them in order to feel valued! It wasn't until the transition from female to male that these hooks became exposed and we began to see their detrimental effect upon us. The confusion we experienced was immense because we knew we loved one another, were committed to each other, had a beautiful relationship and, yet, here it was exploding all around us.

So, although Beatrice set me free to study and develop a richer sense of the self I was becoming, she also was torn between her own needs to feel important and those that would allow me to thrive. Obviously these are not mutually exclusive, but if you have poor self-esteem and always measure yourself against others then jealousy can creep in and you might begin to resent the other person's success.

Beatrice: I didn't realise I was jealous of Wenn; it took many years of constant talking together, analysing our emotions and exploring the issues we were facing before I could admit this to myself. Wenn was so good at connecting the dots and working things out. When something clicked with her, it really did and she was able to move on. I seemed to go round and round in circles! Even when I understood something I still could not readily integrate it into my psyche.

Much later on in our relationship, after several years, I think it helped loads when I went back to Switzerland and saw these patterns in my siblings and other family members. There was always something I learnt. I saw the control issues they lived with and the poor self-esteem that caused them to gossip, or extol the virtues of others more educated and/or wealthy than themselves. These patterns were so obvious to me; these self-defeating behaviours shouted at me. It was like holding up a mirror and seeing the roots of my discontent.

But once I had seen and recognised it, I was left with the need to do something about it. This was easier said than done. During the earlier years of our relationship I had also been diagnosed with autism, anxiety disorder and depression. Being autistic means we are single minded and very literal. When one thought is taking over our thinking there isn't room for any other. I tried cognitive behavioural therapy (CBT) where your thoughts are challenged, but it didn't seem to help much. Many years later I was to discover the art of 'mindfulness' within acceptance and commitment therapy. I found this to be very helpful. Focusing upon my breathing, a single sound in my environment or a fragrance seemed to interrupt some of my obsessive thinking, giving me a break and allowing my thoughts to change course. Of course, this didn't always work!

This change in my thinking, understanding and coping mechanism took years to uncover. It is only happening to me now as this book is being written.

Team work

Beatrice: *When Wenn had the opportunity for a career as a writer and lecturer I knew it was the right thing for her. Her studies continued and she eventually received her PhD in psychology and registered as a psychologist. But she needed me to do all those practical things she* *wasn't so good at. This made us a great team, but it also meant I had to visibly support her, and this was a nightmare for me. I dislike social interaction and find small talk tedious and difficult. Wenn's success highlighted my failures and, although I reasoned it was good for me to have to face the outside world (I prefer being a hermit), it was always traumatic. I felt very angry with her for putting me in this position and I started to drink more alcohol than was good for me.*

I certainly couldn't have managed all the travelling and being organised for the engagements that began to dominate our lives without Beatrice's support. This wasn't just about my career, it was our career. We were a team! She drove our car (I didn't have a licence), took charge of all the domestic arrangements, made sure I had the things I needed and helped with the paper work. Beatrice found my scattiness difficult but came to accept this was part of my being ADHD (a further assessment a few years after the autism one revealed I was living with an attention deficit and hyperactivity disorder), and she knew I tried very hard to finish things I started, but that this was difficult for me.

Beatrice: *Wenn loved to present at a conference or conduct a workshop. It gave her life and was a joy to observe. I never tired of listening to her wisdom and to seeing a light go on in other people as they connected to what she was saying. But for me, although these times were a privilege and I felt honoured to be part of them, they also were incredibly taxing times and took life away from me. It was hard to get the balance right and make sure we had time for each other as well as time on the road travelling to and from speaking engagements.*

In her heart Wenn is a social being. She loves people, activity, being spontaneous and life itself is a sheer joy. I am so very different in each of these respects. I don't want to be involved with people; they are such hard work. I like to plan an activity and take my time over thinking about it and looking at it from many different angles. I dislike being impulsive or doing things on the spur of the moment, and life is a drudgery to get through. So you can imagine the types of conflict we experienced in our relationship, and I think it's totally understandable that lack of control over something was very threatening to me. But on the other hand, I was Wenn's anchor and she, my motivation. During Wenn's transition time, however, it felt like the very fabric to the foundation of our relationship was stretched beyond its limits and was in danger of disintegrating.

It had taken us both such a long time to realise it, but the co-dependency in our relationship was preventing us both from becoming the individuals we were meant to be.

Beatrice: This was a developing awareness that was quite a shock really. After Wenn's transition had begun, the triggers that hooked me into feeling irritated with Wenn and resulted in me being disrespectful were a dramatic attempt to gain control again. I felt as if I were losing my only love! Wenn didn't buy into my patterns of control any more. For example, rather than Wenn sitting with me if I drank too much or if I were giving her the silent treatment, she left me to it! I wasn't used to this and it scared me. I knew I had to parent myself, rather than expect her to do this, but the child within me withdrew me even further and I felt this terrible sense of loneliness.

Wenn's hooks for needing to be needed

Of course, I had my own hooks for needing to be needed. I had grown up in a family who found my 'difference' unacceptable. Lots of family conflict was blamed upon me, or at least it seemed that way to me. I was desperate for my father's acceptance and worked hard to get things right so he would be happy with me. I had no idea I was setting up a lifetime habit that would leave me needy, gullible and open to abuse.

If Beatrice withdrew from me I felt utterly lost and desperate to climb back into her 'good books'. Always being treated as 'stupid' when I was a child and not having connections to my own family had seen me 'over-attach' to a desired other in order to find a place of importance. I loved Beatrice utterly and had to 'get her to love me', no matter what it took. I didn't know how to cope with the feeling of not being wanted and did all I could to change it. But since the transition process had become the established norm, something amazing happened for me. It wasn't just the body changes or the clarity of mind; it was the becoming of my own person. I was learning that I was OK even if Beatrice withdrew from me! It wasn't comfortable and it didn't change my love for her, but it changed my dependency upon her.

This 'need' had been central to our relationship, although neither of us knew it. I needed to be needed, and Beatrice needed to feel important by having the other person need her. This was a recipe that worked for us, until it all changed during the transition; until I changed.

Now, many years later, our relationship is being forged along different lines. We are discovering how to relate as independent people; we are learning what it means to be interdependent, rather than codependent.

Middle sex

My career as a writer and presenter had a solid foundation and one that Beatrice and I had built with much sweat, toil and tears. I thrived on the work and loved my life totally. I came to a place where I began to accept I couldn't be the typical female my body dictated, so I began to use the label 'middle sex' instead. It seemed to temporarily squash my discomfort and allow me to further move away from the feminine and towards the masculine. In many ways this wasn't too threatening to Beatrice because my personhood was still housed in a female body; I looked and sounded like a woman, just one who was rather butch!

For decades I had worn a tie and shirt with my best 'presenting' trousers whenever I had to facilitate a lecture, workshop or presentation. I loved to research autism and uncovered the work of Dr Dinah Murray. Dinah's work mirrored my own. I hadn't found anyone previously who was saying and teaching the same concepts as myself. I taught that autism was about having a brain that found multi-tasking difficult (unless the individual was motivated and this helped them join the dots), but being single focused and having deep-seated interests was the default setting.

At university I also discovered others who understood what I was saying, and many agencies began to book my time to give talks to their staff or to parent support groups. I also connected to other adults on the spectrum and really enjoyed their 'no bull-shit' company! I had found my calling and a people who were my tribe. It was awesome!

But this was my story, and although Beatrice also enjoyed the company of fellow autistics, she always felt 'less than' when in the company of those she considered intellectual.

Beatrice: It's alright for Wenn! Wenn has this way with words and comes to life around an intellectual conversation. I simply freeze and can't find the words to join in at all. I found myself, at times, feeling very frustrated that she put me in this place. I could feel a sense of 'distance' and was sure these individuals thought of me as 'stupid'. They saw me as a person who ferried Wenn around, did her washing and cooking but wasn't able to contribute much in the way of stimulating conversation. It's taken many years of challenging this notion and realising that, at times, 'the professor types' may be intellectually inclined but they are far from being practical in their everyday lives. Appreciating that even the brightest of individuals have their flaws helped me to further accept myself, and the sense of being inferior gradually became less so.

When Beatrice and I questioned why she thought these things it seemed to come from an ingrained poor sense of regard for herself. Again, it took us back to words spoken about her when she was growing up.

Beatrice: *It didn't matter how hard I tried, I was always criticised and told I could have done better. I wasn't bad with figures, but language was always an issue. Eventually I came to appreciate I had an auditory processing difficulty. This means I heard the words normally but my brain took its time to sort them out. Often along the way I lost words, misinterpreted them, took them literally and so on. My family was not aware of my difficulties, but it meant no matter how hard I tried, even with extra tutoring in German, it didn't improve. Unfortunately this also contributed to my poor self-esteem.*

How important it is that children grow in surroundings that allow them to flourish and become who they are in a safe environment. So many of the difficulties we faced in our relationship were not so much to do with true gender identity, but more with poor perceptions of self and negative assumptions concerning our abilities, the expectations upon each other and societal expectation in general.

It's because of Beatrice's commitment to my best interests, in spite of her challenges, that we have a career together. I admire her courage in the face of all the fear and insecurity that dominate her. She is fighting back!

CHAPTER 6

WHEN A LESBIAN IS NOT A LESBIAN

Maybe it was because of our generational years or our traditional view on love and marriage, or maybe it was simply because it was foreign, but both Beatrice and I had lived fairly sheltered lives and hadn't much experience of meeting or being with people who were 'different'. Therefore, for Beatrice and I, 'coming out' as a lesbian couple felt very strange. Also, coming from our Christian heritage and holding the traditional, narrow and naïve values we had grown up with, being 'gay' was still very uncomfortable.

Being a monogamous, committed couple, we were never at home in any aspect of a promiscuous gay scene where individuals seemed happy to mix and match. We didn't frequent gay clubs, didn't march for gay rights and were unsure of gay etiquette at functions where we were amongst other gay people. We were absolutely pro-gay rights and not ashamed of who we were, but somehow for us the label 'lesbian' and being gay just never felt totally adequate. We were definitely not 'anti-gay' in any way but still had a bad taste in our mouths from our evangelical heritage. At first we thought our discomfort was because the whole 'gay' scene was still unfamiliar and all a bit foreign, so it would be a matter of giving ourselves time to adapt and adjust so we could incorporate this part of who we were into our lifestyle.

However, no matter how hard we tried, this didn't happen for us. When we were with other lesbian women we totally enjoyed the acceptance and opportunity to be with people of like mind. We could share our affections easily and without judgement. We could make jokes and comments about the joys of being attracted to women! We could watch movies and television shows depicting lesbian love, lesbian politics and a lesbian lifestyle. All of this, though, did nothing to help us feel more at home as a lesbian couple ourselves.

So, after many, many years of living as a gay couple, I began to adopt new terminology. This wasn't something we talked about or outwardly processed; I didn't tell Beatrice. It was more a matter of slipping into this new state. I kept thinking of myself as somehow caught between two gender worlds. I wasn't female and I wasn't male, I was in the middle. So, I began referring to my gender as 'middle sex'. The more I thought and talked about being a 'middle sex person' who happened to love a woman, the more the word 'lesbian' didn't sit well with me. But even the term 'middle sex' – although initially giving me the freedom to dress exclusively in male attire – still gave me a feeling of being caught in 'no one's land'.

Times of depression coupled with times of feeling at home with who we were and what we were building continued. We moved in and out of those zones. I think we thought it was all a matter of experience and of getting used to our relatively new lifestyle.

Although we missed the church community, we formed new friendships and a whole different world opened up for us. But the disquiet and discord within me continued and it wouldn't let up.

Perhaps to compensate I immersed myself in my studies and the university 'student' culture, which I loved. I became editor of the university newspaper and this occupied much of any spare time I had. I was aware, as a mature student, that I was often out of touch with the issues the younger students were facing. I welcomed them sharing their experiences with me and felt honoured that they trusted me with these.

Despite the age differences between myself and the majority of other students, I didn't feel so odd and different on campus because I was amongst so many other odd and different people! But even there I sensed a dislocation. There were clubs for gays, clubs for women, clubs for men and clubs for individuals with special and particular interests (e.g. chess club, computer club, Australian History club and lots more), but I didn't belong in any of these.

Those years of disconnection from church and our Christian community were strange and difficult. Since my early teenage years I had known life as a committed Christian, and church, along with my family, had been my whole world. Exploring ways to build life outside of the church was unfamiliar to me and I didn't know how to go about it. I still had friends who were originally part of the same church community and who also had left the church and we continued to relate and spend time together. It was just that outside the church framework life was difficult to navigate. For example, church life was structured and operated with set timetables. In general people didn't swear, practised forgiveness, didn't smoke or drink too much and didn't have wild parties! But outside of church life people were not so restrained and not so accepting of Christian ideology. Yet there seemed to be a greater acceptance of who we were and less expectation to conform. We began to see more clearly a picture of the wider human spectrum.

In many ways those years were freeing and fulfilling. We had taken church life for granted and had never considered it would not be a part of who we were. Inside church life were many expectations and set events that were normal and usual: bible study, prayer group, youth group. Church life was a culture all of its own and totally absorbed us.

However, thinking for one's self was not encouraged. Questioning one's reality, emotions, thoughts and experiences didn't happen for us. The leadership team was respected and followed, often without question or much consideration. It's not that questioning was frowned upon so much as it just wasn't given space and time. If we had continued as things were, we may never have discovered our own gifts and abilities, let alone sorted the challenges that faced us. I can see how being free from the restraints of church life allowed other doors to open. This doesn't make church life wrong or stop us missing the community life we were once part of, it's just a truism.

Finding my tribe

It took us some time to build up an awareness of the kind of academic and social difficulties we were living with, but eventually we recognised the right tribe and place for us. I think being part of the autism community replaced the connection to church. Church had given our lives meaning. Our Christian experience, even outside of church life, would always continue to give our lives meaning but it still needed direction. Within the autism community we found a meaning for our existence. Here was a space and place where we each could be 'me' in whatever form that took, while still being able to give to others.

It was interesting that, at many times, my presentations on living with autism were hosted by parent support groups in church venues. I was in one church in a city in the UK that I knew very well. That very church had seen members of my previous Christian family meeting Sunday after Sunday during my young adult years. Here I was, presenting on autism to an audience of more than 200 people. I was standing at a familiar pulpit, with a gold and red sash hanging on the wall behind me. It read: 'You shall know The Truth and The Truth shall set you free.' At that time I remember thinking: 'Yes, Jesus is The Truth; but it's our truth that He is leading us into.'

Uncovering the truth of who we were and the implications for our relationships was a difficult and gruelling experience. Were we uncomfortable with the term 'lesbian' because secretly we believed being homosexual was wrong? For myself, why did I squirm and avoid the touch of the person I most loved in the world? This time was a long awakening that for ages we didn't have words for.

Love making

It was a time when so much made little sense. I loved this woman who was my partner and I couldn't get enough of her, but during our love making if she attempted to touch my chest I pulled her hands away and redirected her to hug me more generally instead. My breasts were a 'no go' zone, and I felt like erupting in anger if she strayed there out of teasing me. But, because I also disliked it if she lingered in a kiss or got too close to my ears, I assumed it to be a sensory thing. I had lots of sensory discomforts and I piled these all together.

I preferred sex to get to the point and failed to see the relevance of foreplay. I knew it was a common practice and need in most women, so I tried my best to carry this on for as long as I could, but it was never a joy to me. Beatrice had many erogenous areas on her body and loved to be caressed. It was as if she was 'joined up' but I wasn't. Sex only occurred between my legs! Being touched in other places only seemed to irritate.

Beatrice: I tried really hard to get Wenn to take time over love making. I could cuddle and caress for hours but she just wanted to get on with it. It was a little different when we were first 'going out'; neither of us could keep our hands off each other and we couldn't get enough cuddling. But kissing was always an issue. I knew it over-stimulated Wenn and I couldn't linger for too long. I never understood the 'no go' zones though. I thought if I teased Wenn enough she would get over it. But she never did. Over time I came to understand much more about sensory discomforts, but it was still hard to accept these limitations when all you want is intimacy with the person you love.

I was also uncomfortable with watching two individuals loving one another. There were often films or television shows depicting couples making love or being intimate. I had to look away when this was happening. I assumed it must be because I saw intimate love as private and not for public viewing. I was amazed, as this totally changed for me during transitioning. I think the hormone testosterone is responsible for this big difference.

When I finally let go of the lesbian identity, despite seeming to fit the profile of one, I found so many more ordinary, human interactions were available to me. This was especially true after chest surgery. Once my breasts were removed and the surgeon had sculpted a masculine chest for me to replace the female one I once had, my nipples were no longer out of bounds for Beatrice. It was an incredible day when I learnt that my experience was a common one amongst trans guys, many of whom couldn't stand to have their nipples touched by a partner. Also, so many of us first attempt to find our home amongst the lesbian community before realising it's not the home we belong in. It's when the light dawns and we wake up to the truth of who we really are that the first chains begin to fall off.

Initially I hadn't recognised that the lesbian identity was further binding me to all that was female. I thought that by being a 'butch' person claiming the ground of 'middle sex' I was becoming freer to be myself. After all, I could wear masculine clothing and enjoy masculine pursuits, and there was a place for this. Being seen as a 'butch' person who enjoyed science fiction, motorbikes and many 'manly things' seemed OK and fitted right in. Yet, the deeper I went with this, the more discomfort I felt. What was happening to me? Why was I not satisfied with my lot?

I don't think I really meant to seek out answers and I wasn't aware that I was searching for something more, but, when I came across television stories or individuals who talked about being a trans person, who had moved from one gender to another, I was spellbound. The more I thought about this idea it seemed the more I came across it in all sorts of places.

On an overseas trip in early 2000 we visited Switzerland where I met Michael for the first time. Another friend had told me that Michael used to be Ruth before he changed his gender identity. Beatrice was in Switzerland to visit with her family and I took the opportunity to meet local Swiss autistic adults while she was with them.

The trip resulted from a previous visit from a young Swiss man living on the autism spectrum who had stayed with us in Australia in the late 1990s. Now we had the opportunity to meet his parents and a small group of other autistics in his historical home in Zurich. The house was on a hill and sat three storeys high. It was more than 200 years old and had a 'Peter and Heidi' feel to it. I could just imagine that once there would have been goats in the lower level of the house; each room still had a fireplace. The meeting around dinner in the dining room, all seated at a long sturdy wooden table, was boisterous and each person had lots to say. Michael was one of the quieter ones and also someone who spoke good English.

Meeting Michael was the beginning of another ongoing friendship that was to help both myself and Beatrice in the years ahead. Michael was amazing. In spite of his autism and sensory difficulties he had pursued gender affirming surgery and was now living as a man. Beatrice instantly admired and trusted Michael. Although we didn't talk much on that occasion, I recognised that I was like him in more ways than just my autism.

Like a death

Since that first encounter Michael and I have met on several occasions, sometimes with Beatrice and sometimes on our own. Beatrice and I are very grateful for his friendship. At times it's been Michael's calm and reassuring manner that has kept both Beatrice and I sane. His wisdom allowed us to take our time to 'feel' the difficulties we would be experiencing in the transition years that were ahead of us. Especially since 2013 his words have allowed us to explore what transitioning means to both of us. Michael explained that the partner of the person going through the transition often suffers in ways they may not even understand. It might not be enough that they love that individual because the person they love is encapsulated in the physical gender they had been used to. To adapt to this change as that gender dies is almost like a physical death too.

Well into our transition Michael told us of other couples he knew whose relationships hadn't survived the transition of one party changing their gender identity. He explained that it's not simply one partner who transitions, it's both. If the lesbian identity was who Beatrice truly was, I don't think our partnership would have had much chance of surviving. It's not just all the challenges of working out how to relate to someone who is changing, even when their personality remains intact. It's about attraction. The one thing Beatrice was sure about was her attraction to the female and her lack of attraction to all that was male. However, the more we explored this, the more she uncovered a romantic bias towards both genders. She had always admired a handsome male physique and enjoyed fantasies about sexual interaction with men, but she only felt she could do this safely while she was loving a woman. Now, she was being challenged in new and different ways all over again. Although it was important to sort out the baggage from the good stuff, it was exhausting!

It's not the kind of topic people engage with – talking about one's sexuality and what the usual ways are that individuals employ in their sexual expression – this was all foreign to us! Gradually, over time, we began to notice it wasn't so black and white. There were lesbians who said they were 'into breasts', there were lesbians who said they were 'legs' people, and so on. We also met individuals who were 'bi-sexual' and related romantically to both sexes. The more we ventured on, the more we became aware that humanity, gender and sexuality did not fit into the neat boxes we had been led to believe in.

In many ways this was a relief because, as my transition took hold of us in later months, it gave us both hope that our relationship could work, even if being romantically drawn to women applied to us both! Maybe we could love one another as people? We were both holding onto the knowledge of our experiences over the past 32 years and just couldn't imagine life without the other.

Maybe it was my naivety, but I really just expected Beatrice and I would always love one another the way we did and nothing could ever change that. Oh, we had times of total frustration with one another; with disappointment and hurt over some trivial misunderstanding or failed expectation. But these times, although very difficult, never truly threatened the security of our relationship.

Change for Beatrice was very threatening. For example, when we had to move house, albeit in the same town, Beatrice refused to pack up and prepare for the move. It was as if she could make it not happen if she pretended it wasn't! A good friend of ours spent the week with us helping me pack and organise for the move. My dreams of us doing things together as a couple took a beating on that occasion, but we survived it.

As I look out at the world through my eyes I see, hear and feel just the same way today as I did 50 years ago. Oh, I have matured in my experiences of life and my decision making is less erratic, but I am still me. The thought of not being me wasn't one I entertained, nor could I. As the idea of a more butch, masculine Wenn grew, it did so without much warning and with my hardly noticing that it was happening.

We both have lots of difficulty coping with change, whatever the nature of that change may be. When I'm on the road as part of a speaking tour, the only constant thing is 'change'.

I give my 'home' routine away, and in its place others direct and inform me of what's expected. I have a written itinerary and this guides me through each day. But for our transitioning together we had no instructions. We had adopted the scripts that belong to being a gay couple; this took much time and energy. We were tweaking this somewhat by moving on to the idea of 'middle sex', but this was still within the gay aspects of who we thought we were.

Now, it seemed all of that might be about to crash land and could end up lying at our feet in an abstract form that seemed to represent a mixed-up trifle that hadn't turned out quite right. Here was I, happy to be the explorer on this journey to self-discovery, but there was Beatrice about to face a mountain she did not feel equipped to climb and wasn't inclined towards because she was sure the view would be a disappointment.

CHAPTER 7

HOW IT ALL HAPPENED

I was at a conference in Newcastle, New South Wales, where
I had been presenting on autism and learning. One of the
team members drove me to the airport after the conference
and, because we had time, we stopped for a cup of coffee. As
we drank our coffee in an airport café, she shared with me
the joys of her previous job. She had been a nurse involved
in supporting 'trans people' after surgery. I looked at her in
amazement. I didn't mean it to happen but I blurted it out:
'I've been thinking of transitioning myself,' I said. She replied
that this wasn't a shock to her and told me I reminded her of
many of the trans people she had known.

She shared with me the joy on her patients' faces as they
became aware of gender affirming surgery and of not being
bound any more to the gender they had previously been
identified as. She talked about gender dysphoria and the
impact it had upon people's lives. She asked me what my plans
were and what I would be doing next. I heard myself tell her
that this was something I was unsure about but something I
needed to investigate.

Beginning to realise I live with gender dysphoria

It's strange, but it wasn't until I spoke those words out loud that the light switched on for me. Here was the truth of the reality that was facing me. The probability that I was someone living with gender dysphoria began to take a firmer hold on my thinking: 'I'm a person with a mismatch between my physical body, the gender it dictates and my feelings of being "all wrong"; I might need to transition out and away from the female and into my true male self.'

My heart was beating so fast, I thought I might collapse! How would I tell Beatrice this news? What would be her response? What would it mean if I transitioned to become the man I was beginning to realise I should be? Would our relationship survive? I reasoned with myself that in the early days Beatrice had wished I were a man. She was uncomfortable with my being a female. It had caused a kind of despair to rise up in her because she was recognising her love for me and the complications associated with this, because I was a woman. But all of that was a long time ago. Things were different now. She had accepted our relationship as a same sex union and, although uncomfortable for her, she was 'out' as a gay woman.

The decision to transition

After arriving back home from my trip to New South Wales Beatrice and I sat together in our lounge and I told her I had something to share with her. She said she had something to tell me too. She seemed excited and I was eager to hear her. So I asked her to speak first:

It was this programme on TV last night. It was all about trans teens.[1]
They each had known they were in the wrong bodies for their gender
identity but, I mean, the courage it took to tell their parents. For
example, one mother was amazing! She wished she had allowed
her 'son' to dress in clothes appropriate to her gender when she
was even younger, like as a three-year-old. Another mum was
really angry and told her son if he thought he was meant to be a
girl he would need to live elsewhere. Over time she came round
a bit and tried harder to accept him as a 'she'. She even took her
(son) daughter shopping. I wanted to tell her that she should be
supportive and accepting. It's not like anyone would choose this. I
mean, why would you?

I was staggered. I could tell Beatrice felt such a genuine
understanding and concern for the individuals she had
watched and their stories had touched her deeply. What
would she do with my news though? I proceeded to tell her
of the encounter and conversation that had captured me the
previous evening. Although she listened well, her face didn't
paint a portrait of welcoming my news. She said: *'But you are*
happy as you are. You found the label "middle sex" and this works for
you. These young people were suicidal and couldn't live with their mis-
gendered identity. That's not how you feel.'

I tried to explain that I had felt so torn, most of my life. That,
yes, I hadn't been terribly unhappy, just uncomfortable and
not sure of why. It was dawning upon me that my discomfort
was due to gender dysphoria and I felt strongly that I needed
to investigate further to see if this was the case. Maybe I was
wrong, but I needed to know. I said I would contact a gender
clinic and have an assessment. Her face was horrified as she
echoed: *'But we are OK the way we are and...you won't have surgery*

---

1   *Coming Out Diaries*, ABC, 2013.

to change your body or take hormones, will you? I couldn't cope if you grew a beard or weren't "you" any more.'

I reassured her that I was pretty sure I wouldn't take it any further than just an assessment, but I needed to know. If the assessment said my discomfort was due to gender dysphoria then I might feel compelled to explore further. I didn't think I would have surgery, but hormones might be a consideration. I did at one point suggest if it was such a threat to our relationship, from her perspective, then I wouldn't follow through with this. Beatrice said she couldn't live with that because it had to be my decision; she did not want to influence me by saying she couldn't cope.

Beatrice: It's weird, even though I desperately wanted Wenn to say she wouldn't continue with exploring her gender and the idea of transitioning, I knew she would go through with it. With Wenn, it's like trying to put out a bush fire with a watering can; once it gets going, there's no stopping it!

It was like I'd dropped a bomb on her. The look of devastation was unreal! I reminded her how she responded to the documentary she had watched and how she knew it was so right for the youngsters whose stories she had listened to; how cross she was with the mother who was unsympathetic towards her child and the way she even cried at their pain. This was all true for those individuals, but somehow Beatrice couldn't accept it might also be true for us.

Beatrice: Somehow, it felt different when I thought about siblings, children and their parents, because you expect parents to unconditionally love and support their kids. But this wasn't that type of relationship. This was US! This was us: a married couple and it's on our turf.

The rest of that evening remains a blur. I was tired from the travelling and from all the emotional topsy-turvy that had gone on in my head. My stomach felt like a lead weight and, rather than this news seeming like it was the final missing piece of a puzzle I'd been searching for, it felt like it was about to tear our world apart.

Beatrice was quiet and distant. She finished off a bottle of wine and took herself away into the sunroom extension of our home. She lit a candle there and sat in the otherwise darkened room, a single shot of whisky to keep her company. I sat with her but conversation was not forthcoming. Eventually I said I was going to bed. She said she wasn't ready for bed. An hour later I came into the room to find her asleep on the settee. I woke her and cajoled her to make a move towards our bedroom. It wasn't comfortable on the settee and she needed to go to bed. Reluctantly she gave in, but it wasn't with ease that I finally got her to bed. This was a scene that repeated itself many times over the following couple of years.

Beatrice: *Drinking and isolating myself was my way of showing my distress... I felt totally alone and helpless. There was nowhere to turn.*

The next morning I began my search to find an appropriate gender clinic in Victoria, my home state in Australia. I read everything I could on gender dysphoria and how it presented. I made an appointment to see my local doctor, a general practitioner (GP), so I could organise a referral for an assessment with a psychiatrist. It was a daunting affair seeing as how psychiatrists had said I was mentally ill and I wasn't sure how my situation would be interpreted. Beatrice didn't stop me, but she didn't want to talk about it either. Later, the following afternoon, she was totally furious with me.

She'd been distant and switched off from me on a few occasions. It was her way of coping, and it was meant to make me realise I was hurting or upsetting her. Then she would try to talk me out of some desired plan or other of mine that she wasn't comfortable with. However, her anger on this occasion was extreme. I said: 'OK, tell me not to do this. Tell me you won't stay with me if I do, and I won't go through with it. Our relationship is the most important thing to me.' But she echoed only that it was totally up to me and nothing to do with her. She would not be held responsible for talking me out of this decision, even if it meant the end of our relationship. I was upset that she saw it as my decision alone. We had always shared everything, and this seemed such a weight to have to carry by myself, but I guess she was right.

Beatrice: *Of course, we have equal rights to what we are feeling. Even though we understand the other's perspective, it doesn't stop the discomfort of how we feel. I don't deal well with change; it's very threatening to me. I can't imagine how I will feel. I was cross with Wenn for what she was telling me. I didn't know what the loss of her womanhood would do to us. In many ways Wenn is looking forward, climbing a mountain towards the view from the top; it gives her joy. But I was looking back at the view moving out of sight; I was feeling lost and scared of potential constant discomfort and change.*

Even though it was clear to me that Beatrice wasn't happy, I knew I had to accept responsibility for my actions and not be moved from this developing understanding. I didn't know what the costs would be to our relationship, but I did know I needed to explore the options that might open up for me, if I was living with gender dysphoria.

So with that in mind I set myself the task of pursuing the course that was ahead for me. In the end, after much discussion and debate, Beatrice said she was 'on board' with me but couldn't guarantee how she would cope. This was a fair summary and I told her I appreciated her support and her honesty.

Beatrice: It was a truly awful realisation. I couldn't talk Wenn out of it. She really was going through with this. It didn't matter to her the cost to our relationship or how I felt about it. Nothing I said or did had any impact. I felt totally powerless. I knew she had to do this and deep inside myself I knew there was no way out of it, but I was so miserable and hated the whole idea.

Wenn organised the doctor's visit to get the referral. I felt pretty numb throughout really. She contacted the gender clinic and, eventually, was told she needed to see the psychiatrist there. It was all a very lengthy process and the months spanned out into almost a year. There were all sorts of reasons why the referral wasn't written! Wenn got really frustrated with the system. Our GP didn't really seem to understand the urgency of it all. Then once Wenn got the referral (it was December 2013) she was told the clinic had closed for the Australian summer holidays. I think I just wasn't coping and didn't want to hear any more about it.

On 28 January 2014, I was finally given an appointment to see the psychiatrist. Beatrice came with me. We had watched an *Insight* programme on television where we witnessed the same psychiatrist talking positively about gender dysphoria and its necessary remedy. He said he usually saw 'patients' two or three times during a thorough assessment to be sure this was the issue that was facing them.[2] I felt fairly confident that this guy would be the right person to see. However, the reality of the matter was not to be so forthcoming.

Despite trying to make an appointment, it was delayed many times. Eventually when I did get one, it didn't go as well as I had hoped. Beatrice stayed in the waiting room. She didn't want to be involved, but the psychiatrist called her in towards the end of my session and asked if she was supportive of my need to explore the issues of living with gender dysphoria. She said she was supportive and knew of my struggles. But her face told a different story. Her voice was shaky and sounded thin and weak, more like that of a child than a grown woman. When I questioned her afterwards she said she hadn't been prepared to be called in and questioned by the psychiatrist. She had taken an instant dislike to this man. I assured her it was a usual thing to do because she was my wife and he was checking she was 'on board' with it all.

Beatrice: I reacted immediately to this man. He repelled me and I found myself feeling totally threatened by him. I don't know what it was about him but I didn't like him or trust him. My heart was pounding beneath my shirt and I felt really upset with Wenn for involving me. I understood when Wenn explained the reasons but I still felt uncomfortable. Our lives were complex enough without all of this stuff happening. This would mean more exposure and more change. Even though I supported Wenn, I didn't know if I could live with what might lie ahead.

Although neither of us felt comfortable with the psychiatrist, I knew at least the process for an assessment had finally begun. When I told a couple of close friends what was happening for

---

2   See www.sbs.com.au/news/insight/tvepisode/transgender

us, they offered their congratulations and a handshake. The whole process of transitioning was beginning to consume me and it was hard to keep it to myself. Although, academically, I understood it would be hard for Beatrice, I didn't have any idea, at that time, of what awful discomforts this process would bring for us both.

Beatrice: Yes, for Wenn this was a confirmation of their acceptance of the direction she was taking, but for me it felt more like a slap in the face. I didn't feel as if anyone was seeing it from my perspective.

Over the following six months I had several sessions with the psychiatrist. It seemed to take forever to go through various assessments and rule out other possible issues. I think it took him this long because I already had a history of mental health issues and of autism. He needed to know my current thinking wasn't born from obsessive compulsive disorder or from a special interest. We went over my history several times and I showed him the photos of myself with my sisters. They were wearing dresses; I was in short trousers.

We talked about my growing up and the tomboy years, my difficulties with feeling at home in my female body, of the 'discomfort' and 'no touch' areas with my partner, of trying to accept myself as middle sex and all the years living as a 'butch' lesbian that just didn't fit with me!

It was hard going and I found it most frustrating that it was taking so long. Some of the sessions took place in the Melbourne Clinic, Australia, where the psychiatrist had his practice; others were conducted over Skype (a computer program that allowed us to connect over the Internet from my home or hotel room).

Wenn aged six years, Ali aged five years and Ann aged four years

During those months of assessment with the Australian psychiatrist, I had to leave Australia to travel to Europe for work. Due to my dissatisfaction with the psychiatrist in Australia, I made contact with one from The Gender Clinic in London. It was 10 May 2014 and what a magic time that was. Although Beatrice wasn't comfortable with coming, she took me to this guy's London office and met me afterwards too. It was a wet and cool spring day, but the sun shone upon us long enough to enjoy a walk in Regent's Park. Beatrice said she had a special feeling about this visit.

Beatrice: *This visit felt incredibly right. It wasn't like the one with the psychiatrist in Melbourne. I had a very strong sense of 'peace' and*

felt like it would be good and useful. I knew Wenn would be in good hands. I met the psychiatrist very briefly before I left Wenn with him. He had something about him that put me at ease in my mind. Wenn was incredibly anxious. The whole trip of getting there, parking the car and walking to the office was so anxiety driven. But once there, it just felt OK.

While Wenn was in the session with him I went for a walk in the park. There were so many different types of water birds and others; it was a soothing and peaceful walk. I just knew Wenn would be alright. When I got back to his office and had to meet Wenn I saw her face as she came out of the time with this man; it was a face of being less stressed and so much more at ease with herself. The psychiatrist had summed Wenn up in the very first extended session and now it was set. Wenn was living with gender dysphoria, the assessment outcome confirmed this for sure. He would write a report outlining his opinion, and in this report he said Wenn (Wendy) would be known as Wenn Barnabas Lawson (Wenn had already changed her name in April of that year) and only male pronouns would be used.

PART OF THE LETTER FROM THE UK PSYCHIATRIST

Ref: SL/dg/Lawson

22 May 2014

I met with Mr Lawson today, 10.05.14, at the GenderCare premises in Marylebone, following his self-referral via the gendercare.co.uk website.

On the basis of this assessment and the information available to me, I would tend to see Mr Lawson as fitting ICD10 criteria for F64.0 Female to Male Transsexualism. I consider his psychiatric history to be demonstrably in the past tense, in this context.

There is often a clinical concern regarding individuals on the autistic spectrum that their gender dysphoria might represent an 'autistic interest'. This tends, on the whole, to be over-diagnosed. In my view, the chronology and trajectory described by Mr

Lawson, particularly in terms of his early childhood rejection of stereotypically feminine pursuits and expectations, is more suggestive of gender dysphoria, suppressed for much of his life as an attempt to compromise within his long-standing relationship. In my own experience, 'autistic interests' in the context of gender tend to occur in much younger autistic spectrum patients.

Mr Lawson has, as I see it, begun to establish himself in a stable male social identity, including within his professional life, and consolidated with official name change.

PART OF THE LETTER FROM THE AUSTRALIAN PSYCHIATRIST

20 June 2014
Re: Mr Wenn B. Lawson

The above Mr Wenn Lawson is a patient under my care at the Gender Dysphoria Clinic, Melbourne. Mr Lawson is a female to male transsexual and is undergoing medical treatment to facilitate his transition from the female to the male role. As Mr Lawson is living full-time as a male, I would be obliged if you could amend your records accordingly to reflect his affirmed male gender. I make this request in accordance with the Australian Government Guidelines on the Recognition of Sex and Gender dated July 2013 (paragraph 21a refers) which applies to all Australian Government departments and agencies.

Beatrice: Although the full reality of this didn't hit home for me, I knew it was a marker on the journey for Wenn. But I didn't take in what it might mean for us as a couple; I respected Wenn for all he had done and determined to only refer to him from then on as 'him/he'. So, even though it set the direction we would be moving in, it could not have prepared me for what I was to feel in the months ahead.

CHAPTER 8

MENOPAUSAL PARTNER AND HER PUBESCENT HUBBY... A RECIPE FOR DISASTER!

A journey of gender discovery

Who Am I?

When looking out upon the world
I see as any might,
The things I notice, boy or girl,
Are captured in my sight.

When looking out upon the world
I feel as any might,
My heart can hurt, ache or break
My senses heightened, set or curled
I live through day and night.

But as you look in upon my world
Your head might judge, your eyes not see
The true reality that makes up me.

Flesh and bone of body image
May not make the man
The clothes I wear, may cause a stare,
My choices may confuse.
But what if she is not I am?
What if he is not a man?

This binary world imposed
Is set by those who propose,
Male and female is set in time
When reality says there's not one line.

Beatrice had made it clear she would support me in the process if I chose to continue with transition but she couldn't say how it would make her feel. She had come to accept this was right for me but she was unsure if it was right for her.

I was consumed with the need to begin treatment. The London psychiatrist had been very clear that for those who wished to transition, hormone treatment and possible surgery was the answer to gender dysphoria. He said there were some who took on the right gender identity for them without making such changes, like hormones and/or surgery. They were able to adopt a different name and insist upon being called by that name and referred to in the appropriate pronouns. I couldn't imagine this for me though. The whole female frame that housed me felt totally wrong; it had to go!

It's a strange thing, but it was only as I embraced the transition process that it felt more and more right. Sometimes when one is at a crossroads and unsure of the direction to take, it's only as you proceed that you come to know if your choice was right or not. The more I moved into the process of transition, the more right it felt for me. However, for Beatrice, the further away from the female I got, the more her discomforts grew. On 20 May 2014 I began the testosterone hormone replacement therapy (HRT) that I would need to take for the rest of my life. At first it was a gel (testogel) that I rubbed into my upper torso. I had to apply this to my body each day, being careful not to rub against anyone within two hours or inadvertently pass the testosterone onto a child, for example. The doctor had emphasised that if I cuddled Beatrice within a couple of hours of applying the gel, I could be increasing her testosterone levels and she could develop facial hair and so on!

I found the whole process to be an interference of my day and I disliked the restrictions it placed upon me. I wanted to be able to hug and cuddle Beatrice without fearing the consequences. So, after about three months, I consulted with an endocrinologist and it was decided I would be given an injection of slow release testosterone instead of continuing with the gel. My voice had already deepened and I was noticing an increase in physical strength.

I documented the journey by making short videos. I wanted to 'notice' my voice changing and the male me emerging from beneath my female overcoat. All through this initial process the Australian psychiatrist and I kept up our appointments. I told him I wanted to have my breasts removed and that I had seen a surgeon specialising in plastic surgery in Melbourne. He was not impressed! He then told me I couldn't have such a procedure unless he considered I was ready for it. He said I had to be on testosterone for at least six months before this type of surgery. Various letters were exchanged and the surgery was planned for about six months after I initially began hormone treatment, pending the psychiatrist's approval.

Late puberty

Going through puberty in my early 60s wasn't the easiest thing in the world. For example, I'd always put colour into my hair, especially once I had begun to go grey. I loved colour, and it was common for me to use several colours such as red, blue, green and purple. This was inspired by the colourful lorikeets (type of parrot) that often visited our garden in Australia.

But somehow these colours felt wrong on me during my transition, so I used one colour only: black.

During those early months it also felt wrong to have a feminine hairstyle, even though my hair was short. So, I took myself to the barber. Not having gone to a barber's shop before, the experience was a bit daunting. I never liked going to the hairdresser, full stop! Being in such a place to have my hair cut and coloured was always strange: so many women having lots of things done to their hair, from placing rollers into it to pushing it up into strange shapes and spraying it with large quantities of stiffening mousse! In the women's hairdresser there were lots of women's magazines and loud music playing out over the local radio. The shop had a strong fragrance to it and they always asked so many questions; I rarely knew what to say, disliked all the fuss and felt terribly out of place!

In Australia at the first barber's visit

Just before 11 in the morning I walked along the busy St Kilda street until I saw the spinning red, white and blue symbol above the barber's shop telling me this was the place. It actually said 'men only' on the door outside. I went in and sat down, as was the custom. No appointments were made here, no fuss and no loud music. It was a smaller shop, with larger chairs, more akin to a dentist's chair than the hairdresser I had frequented in the past. The floor was scarred with a variety of shades of cut hair, making the black and white tiles look messy. 'Next,' I heard a deep voice call. I watched as, in turn, each man waiting left their seat to take up a place on the bigger chair.

'A number 3 please,' one of them uttered. I liked the look of his finished haircut and thought I'd ask for the same.

When my turn came around I walked up to the big chair and made to sit down in it.

'This is a barber's shop, men only,' a voice said quite matter-of-factly. 'There's a ladies hairdresser in the arcade.'

'Oh good,' I replied. 'I'm a man.'

The guy looked at me and said: 'Suit yourself.' Then he proceeded to place a black plastic cape about my shoulders and torso, before retrieving his equipment to cut my hair.

Wenn with lorikeet hair colours before transitioning

I dyed my hair one colour, black, but felt
the need to grow it out and be grey all over

It was an interesting experience. I'd not had any surgical intervention at that time, so I still had a female form; but the strength of my feelings of 'being male' were so strong I felt almost indignant that someone could consider I might not be! The other men in the shop waiting also looked at me strangely, but I took no notice. 'This experience will get easier over time, I just need more practice,' I thought.

Chest surgery approved!

Eventually the approval for chest surgery was given; I was able to say I had been living in my true life experience as a man for more than 12 months, but had been on testosterone for six months. Although I had made my decision to have chest surgery, it was not an easy task finding a surgeon who specialised in working with transgender people, and also trusting, if I did find someone, that they would be the best surgeon for the job! I utilised the information from the Internet and from other trans guys who had undergone chest surgery. However, when I explored the photographs of such surgery, I wasn't always comfortable with what I saw.

Beatrice: Although Wenn had initially decided to have top surgery in Melbourne, he was uncomfortable with the process on offer by the Melbourne doctor. Then Wenn discovered a plastic surgeon specialising, amongst other things, in transgender top surgery, in Brighton, England. We were going to be in the UK for an autumn lecture tour and it wasn't difficult to add on a month so Wenn could have the surgery. Wenn emailed him and requested a consultation. It just so happened that we were in the UK, could see the surgeon at the time and it didn't interfere terribly with the work schedule. Also, Wenn liked the look of this surgeon's work and after meeting him really felt he could trust him. In October 2014 the operation took place.

I was never really mad keen on Wenn's breasts. I can't say what it was about them that was off putting. Maybe because he had breastfed four children and his breasts showed a maternal quality; or maybe because he would rather not own them himself and this reflected upon our intimacy. I don't know. I do know that the thought of Wenn without breasts didn't faze me. I didn't want to see him going through pain and I knew how uncomfortable it would be for Wenn to wear a binder for four weeks after the surgery, but I was up for this. However, at that time I had no idea how I would miss this aspect of Wenn down the track, maybe because it was a huge change or maybe because it was just different?

The changes to Wenn's voice irritated and annoyed me. I wanted to cover my ears and not listen to it. I knew Wenn was excited by the change, but for me, I missed the soft, gentle, more womanly voice I had grown to love. There was also a different 'quality' to Wenn's voice. This manly manner seemed to have robbed Wenn's voice of the subtle compassionate tones he had spoken in before. So, as Wenn's voice began to change, I found it really uncomfortable; it actually hurt to listen to him. At times when he answered the telephone I didn't recognise that it was him. Wenn had always loved to sing; now as puberty set in, his voice was 'breaking' and he lost that ability. It was really strange to hear this change! Also, as the voice became much deeper and his physical strength more apparent, I found myself acting negatively towards him. I was constantly irritated with him and I perceived him as being 'bossy' if he wanted me to do anything. I tried to keep my discontent to myself but I found myself retreating from him more and more.

What we were seeing

I think the transition process was forcing us both to grow up. Testosterone switched off my female tendency towards over-emotive or gentler responses. This placed a distance between words spoken and possible reactions. As we chatted about this together the reasons for the things we were experiencing emerged. It seemed as if the codependency was being broken; the individual 'alone self' was being freed to feel and experience. Beatrice said she used to hide in me, like a child. It was a safe place...but she has never felt safe in male company. She recognised that her need to control me was born from the fear of me becoming too independent and not needing her. Her need to be central to everything in my life was because she had to gain her sense of importance from being important to me. The things I did were a threat to that for her. We talked about her feeling of being 'pushed' out of the nest and how she was being forced to fly.

Beatrice: *Being 'on board' the boat with Wenn was essential because I knew I needed to transition too. I had heard other trans men and a partner stress the importance of being committed to the process if there was to be any hope of making it work. Therefore, if I had allowed myself to give into the feelings of not wanting to do this, the gap would have widened even more between us. I knew this was right for Wenn and my love for him wanted the best for him. No way did I want to stop him from becoming all he needed to be, but there was no time to connect to what was happening for me. At the time I needed to be with Wenn to support him in all the physical changes he was going through, but it didn't occur to me that I needed to make the time to deal with my personal responses. I was totally unaware of what was coming just a few months ahead!*

Inside myself I was running and falling into a deep sense of despair. It felt like being caught up in an avalanche that was sweeping me along, and all I could do was try to hold on! It was many months later, when Wenn was more settled after his fourth surgery (he'd had his breasts removed and a male chest created; a total hysterectomy;

sex reassignment and a micro-penis created from his clitoris; and then his testicular implants removed because his body rejected them, all within 12 months), that the storm ceased and I was taken over by the reality of all that had happened. This was so awful for me; I was hit with the truth of grief and loss in a wave of depression that knocked me for six.

As the days went past Beatrice seemed to be more and more withdrawn, and the deathly distance between us was scary. I had known times of her withdrawal from me and of stormy episodes, but the sun always returned. This just wasn't happening! I could 'feel' that the foundation of our relationship was being shaken. As Beatrice grew further and further away from me I tried over and over to reach her, but she interpreted my reaching out as further demand. As well as the changes to my voice my personal body odour had changed, and Beatrice found this overwhelming.

Beatrice: *It was more than overwhelming, it was phew! He smelt like a guy and it was hard to take this reality in. There was also lots more hair growth on his body, and to cuddle into him was like cuddling into furriness that just wasn't meant to be there! Having my nose tickled as I kissed him and hairiness under my hands from his arms and shoulders, it felt all wrong.*

Whenever we could though, at every opportunity, we talked. Neither of us had a manual to guide us through this time. Transitioning from one gender to another does not come with a rule book. When you learn to drive a car, you are given instructions and can learn from the previous experiences of others. Even when you get married, have children or go through a divorce there are others who support and guide you with what you might expect to feel and experience. During our transition time though, even with all the material that was available online, we found it very difficult to locate the type of support that worked for us. We had very good friends who loved us both, but they didn't have any experience of what we were going through and couldn't be truly supportive with shared experiential knowledge.

The past continues to impact upon the present

Beatrice emphasised again and again that somehow the maleness I lived my life through reminded her of the negative encounters she had experienced with men in her past. These were often fearful or unpleasant encounters, and seeing me kept bringing it to the surface. All that teasing and exposure anxiety! Also, perhaps because of these incidences in her past, Beatrice was very gullible. At times, when I or others had laughed about something, Beatrice felt the laughter was directed at her. These feelings were very, very strong, and even when I tried to encourage her to look at something differently, her suspicions got the better of her and over-rode various other explanations of why someone might be laughing. Down the track though, these were the things that I began to see a difference in as Beatrice faced up to them, challenged her thinking and chose to view her experiences through different eyes.

But until then and sometimes even after, as old destructive habits (the tapes we play) take a time to die, she was still subject to the torment from her past. It seemed the bullying ways of her father, whom she had never felt safe with, and the fear that men instilled in her, continued to forge a widening gap between us. For example, if I asked her something or shared a different opinion to hers, she felt 'told' and bossed about. This reaction to requests from me or of being asked to do something seemed to stem from being bullied by others. If I suggested Beatrice did something, for example 'Hun, would you hang up the washing for me while I peel these potatoes?', Beatrice felt dictated to.

However, from my perspective, nothing about my personhood had changed. I knew my body was changing, but the essential 'me' that it housed was still the same. In the past, to avoid conflict, I had given into Beatrice. I hated confrontation, and I hated being and feeling the distance between us. But now, since my transition, I was my own person in ways I hadn't experienced before and I could think decisively, so at times I voiced my opinion or spoke in more matter-of-fact terms. I never thought of it as being bossy, it was just sharing together as a team in ways that seemed best.

Beatrice noticed the lack of 'something softer' in my voice. Maybe it was the lack of 'beating about the bush' or saying something in a round-about way. Whatever it was, it was interpreted by her as me bossing her around. This definitely wasn't my intention, and whenever she suggested I was being bossy or demanding, I felt really puzzled.

The past experiences with males in her life served to challenge and undermine the transition we were both going through. For some time it was very difficult for Beatrice to separate Wenn from the fear she had of males. The transference onto me of these deeply infused experiences was uncomfortable for us both. For me the good thing was I understood why it was happening; but, although this took away some of the sting, it didn't soften the wounds it caused me.

Menopause

We both realised that Beatrice's mood swings were stronger and more apparent since beginning menopause. We also recognised she seemed more prone to depression and was drinking more alcohol. My transition from female to male coincided with her transition from being a fertile female to one whose periods had ceased. The lack of oestrogen and other female hormones in her body seemed to play havoc with her sleeping, her moods and her general health. I had a feeling that being menopausal also impacted upon her multiple endocrinology (her parathyroid glands were underactive, just as her thyroid gland was), and this contributed to her exaggerated sense of tiredness, lethargy and injustice.

I thought this because I had read an early 1960s paper on the impact of the lack of parathyroid hormone on the mind. The paper had concluded that the lack or loss of this hormone could cause paranoia and psychosis. When we tried to talk to the doctor about this they didn't think there was a connection, but prescribed hormone replacement therapy (HRT – female hormones) in the hope it might stabilise Beatrice a bit more. It might have supported her in some ways (reducing some menopausal symptoms) but it didn't really seem to help very much with her mood swings and her paranoia.

So, this plus the fact that Beatrice was facing elements of her past – growing up in a male-dominant household – colluded to undermine the positives of our transitioning together. My transition was bringing all of this to the forefront. There had long been buried hostilities towards males, but in the past as we mixed mostly with women who were like minded and gay men who were gentle and non-threatening, these issues remained below the surface. Now, it was either face up to them and deal with them or they would explode and cause havoc that would lead to relationship breakdown and separation. However, it's not that easy to work all this stuff out, especially when it's eating you up every day; it was more than simply making choices. Beatrice needed to recognise what was happening to her, and for that to happen she needed space.

At times Beatrice says she still feels lost; like being in a desert without signposts. She can't see any landmarks to help her find her way and is unsure what is expected of her. We need to get to know one another all over again! The very thought of this is exhausting. But it also gives us both hope. Although it's uncomfortable and we are both unsure of how to be, at least we are discovering our footings, tentatively, together.

Beatrice: The further into the transition we travelled, the more I was missing the female in Wenn and I still found myself looking for it in his actions, movements, responses and so on. But I was beginning to see the softer side of being male and this was very helpful. I rejected it at first, and I knew I had a lot of baggage to sort and deal with. But I felt some hope.

We had travelled to Europe for Wenn's work and I was visiting my family. I felt a strong urge to confide in my brother and sister-in-law. The sister-in-law and I were the same age and she was more accepting than other family members; she was also more down to earth. As I told them that Wenn was now living as a trans guy I burst into tears and wept deeply. It all poured out of me and I thought it would never stop. My sister-in-law was very gentle and kind to me, but she was also matter of fact about this and said, 'But you two love one another and are committed to each other; you'll be alright.' Although I appreciated the sentiment, I wasn't so sure she understood my pain.

This was the first time I had told any members of my family and it was a relief that it was out. Their response was encouraging and I tried to take hope from her words.

As time has gone by, little by little, there are changes. These are up and down and not always tangible. Finding words to express what we feel is taking us deeper into understanding.

There we were, gradually building a platform that we hoped would be secure enough to move on from. One morning, as we lay in bed talking and laughing together, as well as having a cuddle, Beatrice commented on the very noticeable differences between cuddling me now and how it was two years earlier. Not only was I slimmer and she could get her arms all the way around me, but the contours of my body created a different feeling for her.

Beatrice: *Your body is so much more muscly and squarer. Even the way you hold me and kiss me is firmer. Sometimes the strength I feel coming from your body is a bit daunting and I still miss the softer, rounder you. But I am adjusting and, if you hold me too tightly, I feel confident that I can tell you. Today, there are periods of time where I feel less confused, less clouded in my thinking and emotions, and can see you and not just the male. Whereas I once reacted almost violently to the trigger of feeling so threatened by the hairiness on your shoulders, now I find myself stroking the downiness of your chest and finding comfort. Maybe it's my way of connecting to the new you and trying to find my home.*

CHAPTER 9

SURGERIES, FURTHER TRANSFORMATION AND THEIR IMPACT UPON OUR RELATIONSHIP AND LOVE LIFE

The HRT (testosterone) was doing its job well but my facial hair was slow to grow and I wasn't always successful in passing for male. I had a flat, masculine-appearing chest, a deeper voice and a male name, but there was just 'something about me' that said 'female' to some people. For example, we were checking into a hotel and the receptionist said, 'How can I help you Madam?' Of course, I corrected her and she was apologetic. I kept asking myself what it was that betrayed me. When talking to a good friend she said that, in general, I came across as a gentle person who had what many considered 'feminine qualities'. She assured me this wasn't a bad thing and that 'time' and 'practice' would reduce the base femaleness that still haunted me. I did all I could to extinguish any 'feminine-ness' that hung onto me, but I also recognised I never wanted to be the male macho type, often associated with dominance.

If I was to be mistaken for a gay male or an effeminate male that was fine by me, as long as the emphasis was on 'the male bit'!

Then there was the experience of seeing myself naked. I just couldn't bear it. Every time I looked in the mirror I saw the female looking back at me. It just felt so wrong! This was kind of interesting though because before the transition I rarely looked in the mirror. Time and time again Beatrice would inform me that I still had breakfast on my face or that I needed to brush my hair. It had not occurred to me that this lack of feeling comfortable to look at myself was connected to the gender dysphoria I had lived with.

As time went by I began to ponder the idea of lower surgery. My chest surgery had been a great success. It still felt tight around my chest, but I came to understand this was because scar tissue loses elasticity and the skin doesn't 'give' like normal skin tissue would. I simply loved the male-looking chest I was left with and I also loved that it was no longer 'out of bounds' to Beatrice.

Despite her irritation and hostility towards me, Beatrice and I still had times of closeness, togetherness and just precious moments. For Beatrice though these seemed further apart and she perceived me to be less and less available. The thing I noticed was clarity of mind and decisiveness in my thinking and decision making. In the past I frequently checked in with Beatrice to ask even minor questions, such as 'Should I take my coat?' or 'Will I need an umbrella?' Now, I was making my own decisions, some not so minor, and not always checking in with Beatrice. For example, she perceived my booking a train fare, after our discussion, as inconsiderate because I didn't re-check it before doing so. This was perceived in general as my not being considerate and not talking to her about things in the way I used to.

Beatrice: It's taken a long time to recognise and sort the differences from our old way of communicating. What I now realise is Wenn has found this confidence that I admire and realise is a healthy thing, but at times I feel threatened by it because of the male dominance issues from my past. If Wenn is firm about a decision or plan I feel less central to the process; this causes me to feel bossed about. So, I talk to myself again and aim to find the balance. I challenge my perceptions of men, male and Wenn.

The trade-off for an even more masculinised brain

The transition from female to male had marked me in many ways that were both subtle and obvious. The obvious ones were my lowered, more masculine-sounding voice, more facial and body hair, broader shoulders and more muscle strength in general. The less obvious marks were those of feeling and being more confident, less 'beating around the bush' (which could be interpreted by others as being less considerate), quicker processing of decisions and conversation in general, and perhaps a tendency to be less communicative of the things I thought and more decisive about actioning them.

These more subtle changes appeared to be the ones Beatrice found the most difficult. My outspokenness and readiness to act on a decision was less likely to be considerate of the difficulties Beatrice lived with. This perceived lack of care for her and the impact my transition process had on her often fuelled the feelings of being disconnected to me that she was experiencing. She would become even more distant from me and move deeper into depression. At times I was very slow to connect to what was happening for her.

Beatrice: This for me was a difficult thing to navigate; Wenn usually takes a while to catch on, but I expected him to know me well enough by now, to read my mind and to know how hard this was for me.

Time to die

Becoming separate people when one's lives have been so intertwined for such a long time can feel like a death. In many ways this has to happen before there can be a rebirth and a renewed coming together as free and whole people. The grief and pain Beatrice was experiencing was as real to her as the loss of one's soulmate might be. I hadn't gone anywhere and I loved her with all of my being, but Wendy was disappearing fast. If I followed through with lower surgery, that would mean all the female aspects to me would be gone; there really was no going back.

Beatrice: I was on-board all the way, for the whole trip. But I was also over it! Wenn kept wanting me to look at various procedures that would complete his transition, but for a long time I couldn't face doing it. The thought of him with a penis was pretty much the last straw.

Lower surgery

When I looked at my body the chest seemed to fit while the rest of me didn't. I had spent hours and hours online searching the Internet for surgeries that depicted gender affirming procedures. I decided that metoidioplasty would be the right one for me. This is a surgery that uses all your own tissues to create a micro-penis and scrotum that then has testicular implants. It seemed the least invasive, and although the phallus would be small it would mean I could stand to pee like any regular guy.

I had shown Beatrice the pictures of such a surgery and we had watched a video of the procedure. I knew it was hard for her to look at those pictures, yet we both felt she, as well as I, needed to have an idea of what lower surgery might mean.

Beatrice: I didn't want to look at the images nor did I want to watch any videos. But eventually I realised the value of doing this and I knew we needed to be as prepared as we could possibly be, for this to happen. I did try talking Wenn out of any lower surgery but I knew it was hopeless. Once his mind is made up, that's it. The videos we watched of the team and various patients in Serbia were really well done. One guy even had the whole thing costed out as well as telling you what was needed for clothing, further places to shop, places to walk, how to use the washing machine and so on. The team were very attentive and patients spoke highly of the care they received. It was clear a doctor would visit daily to check on you after surgery and until you left their care. It seemed the best choice to make.

Although I wasn't comfortable with the plans Wenn was making, I trusted his judgement and I knew the timing was right for him.

I emailed the team in Serbia and expressed my desire for surgery. I had only been on HRT for ten months at that time. The lead doctor of the Serbian team responded quickly. He asked for photographs of the site where he would operate, and my previous trans and health history too. He also needed a letter of confirmation from two psychiatrists to say I was ready for such surgery. These requirements fulfilled the 'transgender international standards of care' that reputable doctors and clinicians were signed up to. Although I didn't want to ask the Melbourne psychiatrist for a letter, I had no alternative.

By the time the surgery would be performed, I would have been on HRT for 14 months. The standards of care required a minimum of 12 months before such surgery, so I was right to go.

Fortunately for me the psychiatrist and his colleague both wrote me a letter after a session with each of them, and I obtained a letter from the endocrinologist too. So, I was booked into the gender clinic in Serbia and the surgery date was set for 28 July 2015.

Beatrice: The reality of what Wenn was doing didn't really come home to me until after the surgery. Up until then I was in a fog about it all and couldn't imagine what it might be like to have Wenn as a fully fledged male, in all respects. So often I still looked for evidence that the female was still present. When Wenn moved his head a certain way or smiled at me I caught a glimpse of the person I once knew, as Wendy. Those moments were reassuring. They told me that the core of who Wenn was, was still there. For me this reassurance was important and helped me to cope.

Before the surgery

As well as preparing to have lower surgery at the end of July 2015, we also had to move our gear from where we had been lodging. Because we spent such a lot of time in the UK we had bought a caravan, which after ten years had to be sold. During our UK lecture tours this had been our UK base and our home. We had a whole home's worth of goods, everything from a microwave cooker to chairs, cushions, linen, cutlery and so on. We were fortunate to have some lovely family and friends who were willing to have these items from us. What we couldn't find a home for we donated to local charity shops.

We then moved into a different temporary home with friends on a hobby farm (smallholding). We took quite a few belongings with us because we thought maybe we would need them. But several months later, in mid-July 2015, it soon became obvious that we couldn't store these any longer and the prospect of needing them again was slim. So, all those items had to be sorted and moved on! It was almost like an omen: saying a final farewell to the life we had lived previously.

Amongst all the packing up and preparations for Serbia we were married at the Nottingham Registry Office, as an opposite sex couple. Due to my transitioning from one gender to the other, our same sex union was no longer valid because we were no longer a same sex couple.

In the UK same sex unions are legal and give couples almost the same status as any married couple. In July 2013 in the UK, same sex marriage was legalised, giving same sex couples exactly the same rights as any other married couple. The first marriage under this Act took place in March of 2014. As a trans guy I wanted to update my birth certificate (so it had my gender as male and not female), which meant applying for a UK gender recognition certificate from the UK authority. You have to have this first before you can request a change of gender on a new birth certificate. I already had a gender recognition certificate for Australia; this is called a 'registered details certificate'.

We also did this because marriage in Australia wasn't legalised for same sex couples at the time Beatrice and I had chosen to formalise our relationship. However, in order to apply for this and acquire gender recognition from the country I was born in, I first needed to change my marital status from same sex to opposite sex.

Us at the registry office where our same sex union certificate was changed to that of a married couple of the opposite sex

This important milestone seemed like a minor event to us because, as far as we were concerned, we were married already! But in reality it housed the enormity of our lives in transition, from one gender to another and from civil union to opposite sex marriage. Even the colour of the certificate was different! Our previous civil union certificate was white while our marriage certificate was green, just like the original certificate I had obtained for my first marriage in 1972!

Getting married (upgrading our civil union) was only a legal formality; it didn't require us to have any special service or ceremony, although we could have chosen to do this had we wished to. Instead we opted for a simple 'signing over' in the registry, which was witnessed by the appropriate people. We were given our 'up-dated' marriage certificate (we actually ordered seven copies) so we had the evidence! I was very disappointed some months later when my application for a gender recognition certificate from the UK was denied. To date, therefore, I still have my female name and gender on my current birth certificate. This causes me much grief and I hope to get it changed in the near future.

After our 'marriage' as a formal declaration, we took ourselves to the North Yorkshire Dales to have a few days' 'honeymoon'. Originally, after our civil union in 2007, we had a weekend away in Dorset, in between speaking engagements while on that year's European lecture tour. We had promised ourselves at that time we would have a longer honeymoon at some future date. But no sooner was our Yorkshire honeymoon over than we were packing for our journey to Serbia for me to have full gender reassignment surgery. Although for me this was a natural progression, for Beatrice it was all moving a bit too fast.

Beatrice: *Wenn took all of this in his stride; but, for me, it only deepened my sense of despair and separation. I followed through with all that was required of me, but inside myself I felt numb. There were moments of connection and even times where I felt a sense of feeling good about it all, but these times didn't last and I'd wake up with a sudden whoosh of reality that served to widen the hole in my heart. I felt wounded and injured and just not right.*

Serbia here we come

On the way to Serbia for lower surgery I saw on a billboard, at Frankfurt airport, a black and white advertisement, I'm not sure what for, but the words written beneath a rugged, handsome face said: 'It's time to transition.' Then I heard the words from the song coming out over a loud speaker as we passed the duty free section – 'I'll see your true colours shining through...don't be afraid...let it show, your true colours...' The thought occurred to me: 'A butterfly needs to be a chrysalis for a while, hidden within some dark tunnel of its existence while it grows in secret becoming all it can be, then it can emerge in all of its true colours.' For me, lower surgery would be the event that allowed the butterfly to unfold its wings so it could be all it was intended to be. I knew that not every person has surgery to unite the different parts of themselves, but this was something that obsessed me and I had to do.

Beatrice: Yes, for Wenn this was the moment he had been waiting for. But for me it was terrifying. There were so many unknown factors. Upon reaching Serbia we were required to surrender our passports and register with the Police. Even the travel money we needed, which was in closed currency, could only be obtained within the country itself. We also had to use it or leave it in the country upon leaving. It was very helpful that one of the doctors met us at the apartment and gave us a mobile phone, Internet access and helped to settle us in, even though it was after ten o'clock on a Sunday night!

We also had a ton of goodies that were familiar foods and vital to our morale. These helped keep us sane. Wenn's suitcase failed to arrive but it was delivered to us the next afternoon. We were told that this was a common issue!

Our first meal in the Serbian apartment

Although we met the team the next day, it was on Tuesday I was booked into the clinic to have the surgery.

The surgery I had was amazing and it allowed me to have all the right equipment that a man could have. My testes wouldn't produce semen, but I had a working penis. It was awesome!

Beatrice: I was surprised and relieved when he came back from surgery; he was all smiles! He put up his thumbs and said, 'Wow, awesome! It's great, babe!' Recovering from previous surgeries hadn't been like this. Usually Wenn was pretty sick and very poorly for a couple of days. It was very good to see him being so positive and looking so well.

157

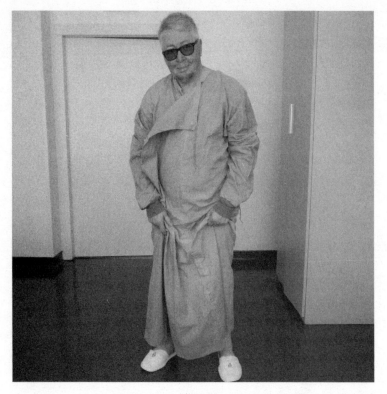

All dressed up and ready to go to theatre!

It was a long and complex surgery and I needed a long time to recover. However, nine days later, just as I was thinking I might be up for a short walk, the wound broke down and a gaping seven-centimetre hole developed. This required urgent attention.

The doctor came to the apartment to collect me in his car. I don't think I clocked the seriousness of the situation. It took us half an hour to get from the apartment to the hospital. When we arrived, a very tired surgeon was waiting in his car for us, the only car in the car park. Under a local anaesthetic, at ten o'clock at night, the doctors carried out their repair. This was an excruciating experience as the local anaesthetic didn't take! For Beatrice, who didn't want to be anywhere else, she had to listen to my screams for over an hour.

During the recovery time in Serbia Beatrice was amazing! She did everything for me, including giving me an injection and, at times, changing my dressings. It took almost three weeks before I could walk normally outside of the Serbian apartment we were staying in.

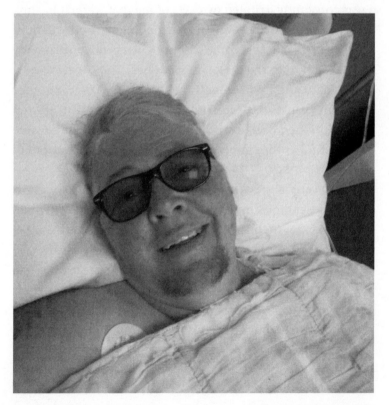

Recovering from surgery

Although all of these events were fitting neatly into our UK tour and holiday times, including time to recover before returning to Australia, they took their toll, and Beatrice, especially, was exhausted. When we finally got home to our Australian bungalow in the Australian spring of early October, Beatrice just needed time out.

A different loss

Although I seemed to be recovering nicely from all the surgery, I was constantly irritated by parts of me that weren't healing as they should. There was this perpetual discomfort and it became apparent that some sore spot was probably from my body reaction to the dissolving stitches. The GP eventually removed some that seemed troublesome. Then, another problem eventuated. One of the testicular implants moved and positioned itself over the top of the other. This became very painful as they appeared to be pushing their way out of my body.

I did eventually lose the testicular implants and this was just one of those things; my body rejected them. I lived with them for several months but eventually one began pushing the other one out. It was quite a business trying to find a surgeon who would attend to me because no one in my state of Australia had the expertise in this area. Gender reassignment surgery was no longer practised in Australia. I did find a surgeon willing to remove them, but he was also adamant I would be scarred and not able to have a new scrotum reformed down the track.

During the surgery I asked the surgeon for the implants. I wanted to keep them as a souvenir but the surgeon wouldn't let me. I felt enormous grief at their loss, something that was quite unexpected. I didn't grieve the loss of breasts or the female genitalia that were taken from me. Not once did I miss these! But the testicular implants had become part of me and symbolised my physical body being joined to my true gender identity. I was quite distraught when they took these away.

Now, as I write these words several months later, I have travelled to India for a (metoidioplasty) lower surgery revision. I'm recovering from the surgery that has seen amendments to the original surgery. So I now have a new scrotum and more masculine-looking genitalia. Since the loss of the first one the micro-penis retreated somewhat and this had left me still looking too much like a female. After all that we had gone through to change this, it was distressing to see this setback, because that's not who I am. When I had the surgery originally, it looked great. I pumped the penis twice a day for up to half an hour to encourage prominence, but to no avail! I needed a revision to that initial surgery because the penis had retracted. The flaps covering its exposure needed rearranging so the doctor could use them to reform a scrotum which would be filled with fatty tissue (mine) and the penis could be drawn forward to become more visible.

Since the original surgery I had experienced times when the dysphoria increased. As a female I had this feeling that other women would realise I wasn't a 'real' woman. I was a breastfeeding freak! I distinctly remember walking through the ladieswear section in a department store and feeling like I shouldn't be there. Looking through ladies' underwear I was waiting for someone to laugh or comment. After the transition, I worked hard to maintain a physical appearance of being male. I grew a beard, had a squarer head and shoulders and hairier legs, arms and torso. But the scar across my chest, beneath where my breasts had been, still betrayed me. It told other men I was not a real man, simply a misplaced female copying maleness! I was afraid of women because they felt foreign to me and I was not one of them. Now I was afraid of men because although I wasn't one of them, I wasn't one with them. I had a micro-penis but it was hidden behind female-looking genitalia lips!

The revision has changed all of that for me. I no longer need to fear men will discover I'm not 'real' and this might lead to ridicule and violence. I will no longer be seen as a fake, a lie. Yes, I was truly never female in my gender identity, but I was, and I am, a mother. Some will still see me as not manly; some will still see the womanly; others will see me as somewhere in between. But I see me as truly and utterly male, and utterly happy with the idea of being a 'man-mum', and this is what counts!

After 22 months of transitioning, Beatrice and I were talking to a friend who asked us how we were doing. The friend wondered if 'coming out' previously as a gay couple was helpful in our coming out as a trans couple. Beatrice's response was one I hadn't expected.

Beatrice: *Not really. Initially I was challenged with Wenn for being female. I had fallen in love with this person, but to own that would mean I was a lesbian. When my mother first asked me if I was gay, I was caught on the hop. I wasn't prepared for this question, and the confrontation overwhelmed me. I wish I had had the courage to own what was happening to me at that time, but the words failed me. I stumbled out with a 'No' and could not look at her. I remember thinking: 'Why wasn't Wenn male? Life would be less complicated!' It took several years before I could tell my parents I loved a woman, which meant I* *was gay. My parents said they had known for some time. But it wasn't just my parents I had to come out to; it was all the family and various friends and others.*

I live with a fear of exposure and all my life I have fought to be accepted. Being gay wasn't what I had imagined for myself! Sure, I eventually adapted and was just happy that I had the love of my life; their gender (being female) wasn't so much of an issue for me any more.

'Oh,' said our friend, 'so Wenn's gender isn't an issue for you and you are not terribly impacted by the change of gender Wenn has gone through?'

Beatrice: *Well, it isn't like that because relating to a woman is vastly different to relating intimately with a man. Although Wenn has always been more male in his identity, it was housed in a female form which was less confronting than a male form. It was only after his transition surgeries, as his chest became physically male and his genitalia too, that I noticed my anger with 'men' was being taken out on him.*

Our friend said we were fortunate because so many couples never got the opportunity to face their demons and work through them, as we were doing. In essence we understood what our friend was saying. We were fortunate to be given this opportunity to work through issues that were affecting our relationship, even previously at a subconscious level. So academically we knew this, but in practice it wasn't how we felt.

Beatrice: *I was aware that I had been given this opportunity but I still felt upset with Wenn because I didn't invite this or ask for it. I didn't feel ready. This kept me in a cycle of 'see and react'. I would see or perceive some male attribute in Wenn and it meant I searched and searched to find some evidence of the 'Wendy' I used to know. Sometimes it was in* *his smile or in his touch. But when I couldn't find any crumbs of that person I became sad and distant.*

I constantly faced a person who was irritated with me. However, every now and then Beatrice responded lovingly or positively towards me. I received a birthday card with HUSBAND written in glowing letters. The card read: 'To The Man I Married...' I was being given signals of welcome while being pushed away. I was beginning to dream of a life that was unfettered by these discomforts:

> ...overlooking the crowded beach. They watched a group of well-muscled, suntanned men working out pretending to ignore the onlookers, mainly women who surrounded them and cheered and whistled their every move. Teenagers sat clustered around radios listening to pop music and there was a serious-looking football match going on over to the left. In the middle of all this noise and activity, dozens of people lay prone on the sand sunbathing, oblivious to everything except the need to get a tan. Far beyond, where the pale blue cloudless sky touched the sea, tiny, white-masted yachts were dotted, apparently stranded on the still turquoise water, and the faint drone of motor boats could be heard as they ploughed through the water, dragging water-skiers in their cream foamy wake.[1]

I'd been reading the book *Stepping Stones* by Maureen Lee. The paragraph above evoked connections to a positive, carefree existence that placed me in the middle of a happy, healthy life-giving place that called me every now and then, and still does. It's a timely reminder that these exist and are real, not

---

1   Lee M. *Stepping stones*. Londo, Orion, 1994, p.37.

just imaginary. It also, somehow, affirms and confirms my own thoughts, dreams and ideas that connect me to some internalising life flow. I might read a book, watch a movie or listen to a piece of music, all of which touch a place inside me that I often can't explain. The problem is, I find I'm losing a sense of 'me' at times, and being surrounded by all that's negative and critical robs me of life. I need to find a way to love but keep negativity off my skin. It rubs and wears away at my body, causing me to feel sore and then numb. It's almost like being dead; it protects me in places but then I slip too easily into a place of despair and find it hard to breathe life in again.

Whilst in England, still on tour at that time, I was sitting having a cup of tea and listening to the rain. There in that springtime the birds were singing in the distance and their urgency for life filtered through the smoky, drizzly rain as it relentlessly dripped and was blown across the courtyard.

I absolutely adored Beatrice, longed for her and spent the hours of my day attempting to 'spark' her up or channel her put-downs. Some days she seemed to benefit from this and returned my smiles and warmth. But there were too many others that kept her locked away in a cold, distant cave and threatened to swallow her very existence. I felt there must be a way to love and encourage her while keeping my head above water, my body alive and my heart from becoming a corpse.

It was May 2015. Two days previously I had returned from the Isle of Wight after three days away with work. During the time away I had stayed with friends, a naval man who ran the local yacht club and was committed to the well-being of his eldest autistic son as well as being determined to build a positive future with his family, and his wife, a beautiful and brilliant local artist who captured life with every stroke of her paint brush and was equally committed to life. Here were two full lives who valued sharing their love, home and heartaches with me. It was an exchange of life-giving values focused upon what might be...and it fostered hope.

When I returned on the ferry to the mainland and then the train from London, I was eager to see Beatrice again. I waited in the cold wind for ten minutes before she arrived. Once inside the hire car I kissed her and smiled. I felt disappointed she hadn't been there to meet the train. I thought about if it had been the other way around... I would have been there early, eager to greet her. I knew parking was an issue and there was just a drop-off zone, but others had their loved ones waiting for them.

Beatrice: I actually did get there early, too early. Because it was only a drop-off zone I decided I'd use the 20 minutes I had to go to the supermarket. But I got stuck in the traffic and decided to turn back, never getting to the supermarket, and this made me late. I didn't intend for this to happen; it was unavoidable. When Wenn got into the car, I was already annoyed at the whole palaver and was pretty defensive. I also felt guilty for not being there to meet him. As a way to assuage my guilt I passed the buck and said to myself, 'Oh well, so I'm late. He can wait.' This type of thinking was very much resident in my family of origin. If things went haywire and didn't go according to plan, in our family there were always others to blame! Once this thinking was set in motion it was very difficult to change it.

Later that evening the iciness returned to Beatrice's face. She spent several hours drinking and was unhappy with the dinner. Many small steps of separation continued throughout that evening and the following day. By night time the following day she was very distant and unavailable. Each time I reached for her, in spite of her distance, I kissed her neck and cuddled her frequently. She responded coolly. Throughout the second evening she drank glass after glass of alcohol. The darkness of night descended and she unloaded her disrespect, disdain and disgust upon me: *'You chose this transition, though you knew it put our relationship at risk,'* she said. I replied I had understood she was very anxious and uncomfortable and unsure of how it would affect her, but she was 'on the boat' to use her words.

Beatrice: *Reflecting upon that time, there were so many subtle changes that were occurring but it was hard to put my finger on what they were. It just all felt so different. I know I took it out on Wenn but I honestly couldn't see anything else at that time. It felt as if Wenn was the one responsible for my pain.*

The atmosphere deteriorated as the evening wore on. Beatrice kept saying how much I had changed; I was less romantic, less spontaneous, less bubbly. Oh, I was the same in some ways, yes, but more 'male' now and less emotionally present. I didn't listen like I used to and she felt 'told' what to do. My behaviour made her want to kick back at me and she felt a growing distance was developing between us. I tried to explain calmly that, yes, I was different, but I loved her deeply and my confidence just meant I was more decisive rather than less available. We were two different people viewing the contrasts of the same picture and seeing it from very different sides.

She poured herself another glass of alcohol. Her mood darkened even more and she heaped coals of discontent upon me, stating over and over again that 'I had changed'.

Beatrice: When you say those two words, 'Love you', they don't mean much. I'm sure you mean them but you just return to your computer or your work...there is no action.

I said that I needed to work, that I loved my job, that she was very important to me but I still had to do things.

Beatrice: I think this kind of transference comes from how I was treated as a child. If I'm not central to the person I love, I feel less important and less likely to connect to them. For years Wenn had said words like 'I love you; you are my life; you are so important to me' but I always found words difficult to process or relate to, unless I had a corresponding feeling. I always needed to look for evidence in the way that corresponded with my expectation. It was to be months later that I began to have a deeper realisation – to the previously academic awareness – of the fact that my whole life of 52 years had been misguided by established core beliefs. These beliefs stated that my value and importance come from my achievements and tangible proof; without these, words went in one ear and out the other!

She echoed that I never used to be like this; that she wasn't coping with the changes and just couldn't relate to the 'male' in me. I said she had looked at me and told me she found me handsome and liked what she saw; that being male suited me more than being female; that, somehow, my body fitted me more. She agreed with these sentiments but said she had had enough and wasn't coping. I asked her what had changed. Had she not meant what she had said? She part smiled and part shrugged, and replied she probably did at the time.

Beatrice: When I read the above I think yes, you are not getting it. You are thinking like a man, and I am a woman with very volatile emotions. I am reacting to you and I will say this stuff out of my reactions.

During the above discourse I had to frequently ask her not to speak so loudly...was it the alcohol talking, or did she really detest me? Eventually I said I needed to leave and would come back when she was more amiable. I moved from the room to a different part of the house where we were staying. She told me to 'fuck off'. This was not the way Beatrice usually spoke.

Beatrice: I spoke to you in utter disgust. Something boiled up inside me and I simply reacted. The maleness you showed called this forward in me. I know it's not right, but at the time I was not concerned about that.

In the past I would have reacted to her hostility by leaving; it was my way of coping. I was never good at confrontation and avoided it at all costs. But since the transition I was finding I had more courage, more clarity, and I was less reactive and more in control of my own emotions.

After a while I returned to the room where she was sitting. I asked her if she was finished yet. She said, 'Yes, I'm sorry.'

I moved onto the couch beside her and we re-entered the conversation. Her venom was apparent and, in the end, I conceded defeat until it was after midnight and time for bed. Once in bed, I placed my arm around her and kissed her head. She seemed to warm towards me and our cuddling turned to caressing her breasts and kissing her. She had no interest in pursuing our intimacy any further but seemed settled enough to go to sleep. I sensed, for this evening anyway, the battle was over despite the continuation of the war between and within us.

This new chapter of our lives was as long as the river that runs to the sea. Its 'newness' was more about the apparent reality as we camped along its banks. We knew it had always been there, but in the past had only caught glimpses of it from a distance.

Now, it flowed between us constantly. Sometimes like a fast-moving torrent that took everything with it, sometimes as a gentle, relaxing stream that offered peace and tranquillity as we bathed in its shallows. But always, it ebbed away at the banks of our relationship, causing them to surrender. I knew some of the rubbish it took away was useful, necessary and opened new channels for communication. However, it was the other wider chasms that worried me. Would these eat away at the love we shared until it was all gone, or would they serve as vessels to hold even more love than before? I didn't know the answer.

Later that week we sat together watching a new TV series; her laughter was infectious. How good it felt to hear her laugh and feel the curve of her shoulder as she nestled firmly against my forearm. The very smell of her was intoxicating and I longed to feel the rest of her body against mine. 'Skin, I miss skin,' I thought to myself. 'I miss her skin and the intimacy of lying together.'

It wasn't new, this lack of desire for sex; it was something that had always dogged our relationship. I was the one who had the sex drive, she often reminded me. The trouble was, it was much stronger, though I hadn't thought it could be, since my transition. Yes, I could take care of my own needs and I did this, but it didn't replace my longing for her.

If I asked for time together it was interpreted as: *'So, your male ego needs satisfying.'* Sometimes she said: *'I'm happy to be cuddled and I'd love a massage; but I don't want sex. Your demands turn me off.'*

There it was again, 'my demands'. 'Why is it demanding to want to have the woman I love?' I often thought to myself. I felt almost resentful of the desires that welled up inside my body. 'But,' I would then debate with myself, 'wanting love and sex are normal, healthy; wanting the love of your life and the intimacy between you that comes with being a couple is supposed to be a good thing. Why oh why does it feel like a bad thing?'

There had always been those times of not wanting me, of my attentions being seen as 'demands'. Somehow I needed to find a way to embrace who I was, and who she was, while not becoming resentful or turning away from her in search of someone who would join me in finding mutuality.

My thoughts were cut short as she entered the room. *'It's the shirt,'* she said. *'My Dad and brother, they always wore those kind of shirts. They just remind me of the injustice, the put downs. My brother was the golden boy, we girls couldn't compete. I react so strongly to "maleness" and I think it comes from the days of growing up never feeling like an equal and, my Dad, he was so rough and so cruel. I know this was when I was older, but it's all the same; his big hands and his ways. My brother got to borrow the car, but if I asked for it, well you'd think I'd asked for the moon! You are a trigger. It's as if "male" triggers both: the drawing towards you but also hostility and a pulling away. There's an anger that threatens safety for both of us. Males are not safe to be with.'*

Being true to self

I wanted Beatrice in my life, but I also needed to be true to 'myself'. Maybe the anxiety of needing her acceptance was related to a fear that hindered me from being true to myself. My self is saying: '...but this is who I am. I am generous, outgoing, needing to connect and be social with this/these people.'

This 'myself' is in conflict with the 'myself' who is being told he cannot do...or be...because it reflects on the 'myself' of the other person (my partner) who lives in fear of having 'stuff' used against them. Stuff such as one's words (they are listening and they can hear your words, which may become gossip and be used against you in some way) or actions (if you visit that place they might think...). The other 'myself' has beliefs that money should be saved and not spent. That 'myself' uses measures to control 'myself' (me) by saying things like: 'You have a different relationship with money...you just spend when you want to...'

Their aim is to manipulate your 'myself' to help their 'myself' to follow through on and support their paranoid beliefs. If their control fails it ups the ante on their paranoia and they will then try harder to manipulate and control you to gain a feeling of control again and reduce their paranoia.

This same strategy is being used in the arguments of the difficulties with 'myself' in this transition or unveiling. Living with a female overcoat on, covering up the male gender identity that has been obscured or hidden for decades, has now stopped and female to male (FTM) full transition has happened. This has necessitated using large sums of money which the other 'myself' has hinted at...then there is their grief over the loss of that overcoat. Grief is real and needs to be appreciated and understood. There will come a time when that grief moves on. But it may take a while, because for the other 'myself' it serves as a strategy to keep things from changing.

Beatrice: I think the projection of male disgust is because I feel trapped. It's in my face, I feel like I have no choice. This fuels my hurt... I could walk away but Wenn is too important to me. Our friend said, 'Wenn has no choice, a plant must grow towards the light to become all it should be...an awakening you can't struggle against...', but where does this leave me?

After the focus on me and all the surgeries had calmed down there was more time to reflect and connect to some of the issues that rose up like hurdles along the course of our relationship. In any race individuals can practise their running and prepare to jump over specific hurdles that they know are there. Unfortunately, the hurdles we had to navigate were unexpected and we could not prepare ourselves for them. Oh, we took a jump at them and did our best, but this usually ended with us landing in a heap!

Time for Beatrice

In April 2016, nine months after my original lower surgery, Beatrice came to a crossroads. She knew she wasn't coping, was suicidal and had to act. A psychiatrist from the Melbourne Clinic suggested using a procedure that was having a positive impact upon individuals living with depression. In spite of her fear of change, her discomfort around people and her dread of 'the unknown', she accepted the offer of this intervention which would see her in hospital for a month, with follow-up treatment thereafter. The treatment was called repetitive transcranial magnetic stimulation (rTMS) and uses magnetic waves to increase brain plasticity and help the brain open up to fuller connections.

The rTMS treatment and other interactive therapies (such as acceptance and commitment theory (ACT), mindfulness and cognitive behavioural therapy (CBT)) worked their magic upon Beatrice. It was quite an adventure for her. There were days of crying and feeling locked in with no way out, then there were days where it seemed the light had been turned on and she no longer sat in a darkened room. The treatment opened up closed doors and allowed Beatrice to build connections to understanding herself; these had not been available to her before.

Beatrice was close to a full-on 'break down' as she was not able to handle life any more. It wasn't just the depression though, it was everything. Coming to terms with her loss and letting it go so she could steer her way along the course we had chosen was proving much more difficult than we had anticipated. In the hospital, the rTMS seemed to be productive. It was hoped this would help her to build a more positive mood and also equip her for further challenges.

We put our girls (the cats) into the cat motel and I stayed nearby at a friend's place in St Kilda so I could be close to the hospital. Beatrice found the experience helpful but scary too. Having to share her thoughts, fears and hopes with a psychiatrist and other members of the hospital team was very hard for her. There were lots of tears, grief and difficult moments for her, but also lots of connecting to positive emotive times too.

It was very difficult seeing her pain and not being able to 'fix' it. She says now that my transitioning from FTM has made it worse and that she has experienced lots of grief over the loss of who I once was and of its impact upon 'us'. The bottom line is that she is now reminded of 'the male' in her experience every time she looks at me.

Her disgust with all that's male (the traditional thinking of male, macho, dominant, patriarchal and so on) is evident and she alienates me because of this. When I say to her that being 'male', although dressed in a female overcoat, has always been me, she says she knows this but still feels like the female overcoat kept that 'male/me' at bay. Even though she knows

I'm not the kind of male who is macho, she still looks at me and sees a man; this is very distressing for her.

Beatrice: It's one thing having male friends and associates 'out there' but it's another having the very thing that has caused so much pain and hurt living right with you as family.

It didn't seem to matter how I tried to say 'that's not me'. Beatrice said this confirmed to her that I wasn't hearing her, that I wasn't listening. I tried to understand her perspective, but I think I switched off from it all. Maybe my reaction was a form of protection for myself. I was unsure. I did appreciate I was not so easily prone to responding to her need to control me as I used to be. I'd become more of my own person since the transition and I believe this was a threat to her. What was becoming more and more obvious was that our relational style had changed.

My love for Beatrice has never been in question. I love her more than words can say and I only want the very best for her. I am hopeful she will work through the male hatred stuff, forgive those in the past who failed her and find some healing; then, maybe, we can move on. I don't know what the next few steps will be or how we will negotiate them, though.

I do know Beatrice is practising the use of mindfulness and ACT in her daily dealings with anxiety, fear and paranoia. Acceptance of who we each are involves understanding what drew us to each other in the first place. Yes, there were components of codependency, but our being drawn to one another was also based upon mutual attraction, shared values, respect for each other and a desire for the other's best.

We both understood the transition time was all about bringing the truth of who we both were to the forefront.

Maybe the 'male' that was being hosted by the female being I had appeared to be was also part of the initial attraction, despite it being covered up. Although it was terribly scary to let go of the codependent aspects of our relationship, we needed to do this if we were to share the joy of being joined to the core of the person we both were. Each of us was so much more than our physical sex or cis gender implied.

CHAPTER 10

TWO YEARS PLUS ON TESTOSTERONE

Just over two years on testosterone and, honestly, I'm still going through puberty. Although my voice deepened very early on, the changes to my body shape and fat distribution (so I look more male and less female) are still happening. My hips are not as wide as they once were, but the tops of my legs still carry too much fat. I never really suffered with acne, which is a relief, but I get this overall irritation and 'itch' that means I feel the constant need to scratch! I think it's the body hair growing but I'm not sure. Beatrice is happy that my lips don't seem to have changed. I've read that sometimes the lips can become thinner; the hands and feet can change a bit too. My head is definitely 'squarer' and less rounded!

In general I'm still taking on the shape and character from the various surgeries I've had. The scars along my chest beneath the nipples haven't faded as much as I want them to. Some guys develop hairy chests and the scars disappear amongst the hair, but this hasn't happened for me. I might get a tattoo to hide them! I tried laser treatments but it didn't help much. Some of it will be a matter for time to fix but I will never lose these scars.

Triggers

Beatrice and I continued to have this thorn in our side: the thorn of my maleness triggering her disgust. Being together was constantly being undermined by some male mannerism or some communication that was misinterpreted. It felt a bit like I was knocking my head against a brick wall and I just couldn't connect to her on the other side. Maybe this is a common feature of puberty and maybe it's a natural part of growing up.

Beatrice: I could see I was hurting Wenn and I kept asking myself, 'Why?' One night as I pondered upon this I recalled how my father signed his name on a letter from home. Usually Mum signed on his behalf. Why would his signing this time make such a difference to me? I think it was because, for a moment, I felt important enough to him for him to bother. Somehow Wenn's maleness triggered my lack of importance from all those childhood experiences when Dad failed to acknowledge me. This might sound trivial, but I understood why I was transferring all the disappointment and failure of recognition I needed from my father onto Wenn. Now, I needed to work out what I could do about it! I needed to sort out what was transference, what was actually Wenn's stuff that I found difficult, what was related to the transition and how to keep my reactions in check as I worked through these things.

I knew I reacted towards Wenn's choice to fully transition and I resented this. But I also loved him and I felt caught in the fog of confusion that clung to me like a wet woollen blanket.

It seemed to Beatrice that she was locked into a relationship she didn't choose and with someone who was walking a path she didn't want to go down. Each time she accompanied me we ended up turning down a side street that saw us meet face to face with conflict. Eventually she decided she could no longer run from this conflict but she needed to look it in the eye and defuse it somehow.

It's now more than two years since I began taking HRT (testosterone) and nearly three years since the beginning of my transition. The physical, mental and emotional changes and challenges have been many and I'm pretty sure we are not out of the woods yet. I know people mean well when they offer their congratulations, but often these feel a bit like empty words. The costs have been enormous. It's hard to appreciate these costs ahead of time because there is no way one can truly know what they will be. One person (Wenn) gets what they wanted; the other (Beatrice) loses what she had.

Beatrice: *Everyone is focused upon Wenn. I feel the difficulties I live with are pushed into the shadows. Coming out as trans seems easier in some ways than coming out as a gay person, but there are still many discomforts. I get to call Wenn 'husband' and 'he' rather than 'partner' and 'she'; this is less exposing for me but still very strange and foreign. For many, many years we had built our lives together as two 'gay' women. We lived an alternative lifestyle, far away from the conventional heterosexual world. Now, at times, it felt like all our history had gone. I'm not ashamed of being the wife of a trans man, but I battled feeling the discomfort of public exposure as a partner to a gay woman. I still mourn what is lost. I felt as if I had lost Wenn and, although cognitively I know that to be untrue, I'm still coming to terms with both the grief of loss and the reality of what I have gained.*

I still have Wenn. We are still together and, in spite of the trauma and discomfort, his love for me remains unchanged. Sometimes when a person recognises they are trans and travels through the transition process their sexual orientation may change too. I feared Wenn might not be attracted to me any more or he might be attracted to men, or be into both! There were lots of things Wenn needed to figure out so he was studying men and maleness and did things I'd never seen him do before; this was very unsettling.

I like the fact that Wenn is slimmer and a healthier weight, even though I accepted he was a bigger person in general than in the earlier days of our relationship. I know he tried hard to stay healthy, but the physical disability he lived with posed limits on exercising and it was difficult for him. These days this has changed for the better. I like seeing him more emotionally and mentally confident and capable, even though this is a challenge for me at times. I also feel warm at his increased strength, but at times I miss the softness of the woman he used to be.

I so wanted to find a counsellor or some individuals that could help us as we shared our story, but even though we were both seeing a counsellor it was difficult to find the expertise of someone working with couples in our situation. I watched video story after video story of different individuals going through transitioning from one gender to another. I searched the Internet to find stories that were a bit like ours. I did find one video blog that depicted aspects of a similar experience. The guy in the video said things like he hadn't known he was trans and it was a gradual awakening. This was good to hear because so many others were saying they knew from early childhood, but this wasn't me or my experience. I had always had this void inside of me, this discomfort, but I didn't know what it was. I couldn't name it until three years ago; I was then 61 years old.

So, yes, I could see Beatrice's point of view. If I hadn't been terribly unhappy and had managed to live my life for more than 60 years, why suddenly was it not OK? Why did I feel compelled to transition from one gender to the other? The answer was that this wasn't a sudden connection but more a gradual dawning. All the time whilst I was in the dark I didn't know the source of my discomfort. There was this constant nagging and pulling away inside of me that I didn't understand. When I'd spoken of it in the past others had said, 'Well, being female is a spectrum too. Not all of us are girly, we don't all want handbags and pink bed linen.'

I knew what they were saying. Yes, it's true that gender is as varied as the stars in the sky. But with regards to feeling 'I don't want you to touch my breasts!' and 'I'm not comfortable using the Ladies toilets', sure, I can live with these things – but why should I have to if there is an answer and a way to get past them?

It's not to do with Beatrice not being important to me or choosing not to consider her wishes. She is the world to me, and my love and commitment to her are unwavering. But surely my love comes from a heart that is torn and not whole? The foundation of our relationship isn't as stable as it needs to be because it's built upon a lie and a codependent neediness that threatens who we each are. In order for this to be rectified, we must both transition into healthier, more whole individuals. To give life to each other we must first possess it ourselves; in the past we have borrowed life from the other rather than building it ourselves. This is a shaky place to relate from and, ultimately, is not sustainable.

Meeting others

I had almost given up on meeting any one locally who was going through the same or similar things to us. I had heard of this guy who was a friend of a friend and hoped I would meet him, but each time it looked like we might meet up things happened and the meeting failed to take place. On this occasion, however, he called in on our friend while we were there, so we introduced ourselves. Beatrice liked him straight away and felt safe with him. He was able to empathise with what she was experiencing and homed in on the particular difficulties concerning the changes. He said not many couples stayed together after one of them transitioned from one gender to another and he encouraged us to focus upon the things that we loved about one another and talk openly about the things that were hard. He admired Beatrice's courage and complimented her upon her decision to stay 'on board' despite the rough buffeting of the waves against the sides of our boat.

Since that first meeting just a few months ago we aim to share together as regularly as possible and feel totally at ease with each other. Nothing we say fazes either of us, and I think the openness to be ourselves, however negative, is freeing.

Male privilege

In many ways, for my life to change and to establish a firmer foundation, transitioning from female to male had to take over my life. It was all I could think of. I needed to find others who had stories like mine so I had some benchmark to follow, otherwise I was left with: 'What if this is just an obsession? What if it's born from wanting to be male because it seems to be easier if you are a man?' I even had one friend ask me if I was doing this to gain male privilege. This really freaked me out! This was turning my world and Beatrice's upside down. It threatened all we had known. I couldn't see any 'privilege' associated with it but more a loss of status.

My beloved despised me at times and there was no way, at the age of going on 65, that somehow more doors were open to me now. Some trans guys say they notice life as a male affords them more choice and people treat them differently, but they are younger, taller and more good looking than me! Jesting apart, I get what many are implying; but no, I'm not going through all of this pain and difficulty to gain access to male exclusivity. I'm doing this because it is the treatment for my broken, wounded condition. It's what is making me whole again. It's allowing me to fully transition into the truest sense of the person I am.

At last, these days, I have grown enough facial hair to successfully 'wear' a beard and decent sideburns too. At last my voice seems to be less scratchy and more constant. I would so love to have the deeper pitch to my voice like my father. I loved his voice! He could sing beautifully too. When he led the singing of 'Oh Danny Boy' just before 'last orders' were called in the bar on a Friday night, the whole bar joined in and it was a joy to behold!

Sometimes I try to imagine what he would make of all this. I would like to think he would understand and accept me as the son he always wanted. Although I will never know, I like to act as if this were the case. I knew my father rarely understood me but he always supported me and I always believed him to be on my side. He had my best in his heart, no matter how that presented. He is one of my role models and will always be my hero.

Being on HRT for more than two years now has produced other benefits too. Whilst some may put weight on, I have lost it. Before I started the hormone replacement I weighed 96 kilos (over 15 stone); today, I am 75 kilos (over 11 stone). My body is generally fitter and I am more able than I used to be. It's not just muscle strength that has increased (relatively for my age) and I'm no body builder, but I can walk up and down stairs easier, negotiate hills on our walks better and walk further than I used to. Although I still live with arthritis and battle the difficulties this presents, I'm just a happier person!

Comfort eating

Another factor is my appetite and desire for various foods. I've always had a sweet tooth and loved desserts and so on. I had to have breakfast not long after I woke up or I just felt very wrong. These things have changed. I no longer have sugar in my tea and eat less in general. I rarely have breakfast before 10 o'clock in the morning; I am just not hungry! Common sense would suggest it should be the other way around; men need more calories and not fewer. I can't explain this change, but in the past food was used as a comforter. The worse I felt, the more I ate. Now, I feel so much better about myself, and I'm not drawn, when I'm upset or frustrated, to using food to console myself any more. Instead I can reason with the problem, feel a bit removed from it and not let it control or dictate to me. Being male in my body and in my mind has reduced conflict for me, created a sense of wholeness and lessened the emotional responses I once had.

Maybe this is one of the differences Beatrice has noticed but may not have had words for. Because I'm less emotional, less defensive and more logical and clearer in my thinking and reasoning, it could easily be interpreted as being less connected, less invested and too black and white! This might directly confront the relational styles we once operated from.

Wenn, Beatrice, grandchildren and Mum, during
my bigger years before testosterone

Beatrice: *I think this is the case. The more we journey together the more
I see where we have come from and what we are heading towards. I
don't always want to look at it and I still miss such a lot of who we were
in our past. But I'm beginning to have a safer sense of our togetherness.
There are days I am not as triggered by Wenn's maleness as in previous
times, and I react strongly if someone mis-genders Wenn. I feel outraged!
To me Wenn is so definitely male and it seems all wrong that someone
might refer to him as a her!*

*It's strange to have been in this conflict. Academically aligned with
Wenn's right to be trans and being 100 per cent with him, but emotionally
missing the womanliness. It was my own personal conflict with
the change we were going through that kept the discord raging within me.
Maybe the positive media coverage of all things trans and the exposure
of all we had travelled through together plus the inner personal conflicts
I was going through helped us understand the drawing towards and the
pulling apart.*

Wenn with granddaughter Holly at the beach after 19 months on testosterone

We have come to understand that we need to build a different relational style born from the foundation of two mature people giving to each other from wells that are fuller and not half empty. But this reality is easier said than done. Communication takes time to set up, especially when it's coming from a changed location, and possibly being delivered via means not previously understood. Decoding the expressions used and separating these out from intentions, metaphorical speech, jest and other types of communication might take some time to establish. But it's a work in progress!

CHAPTER 11

ACCEPTANCE

*B*eing accepting of all the transition-related issues is a process rather than an event. I think it's one reason it's called 'transition' because this implies a process over time and not a sudden arrival. There probably will be a time when we feel like we have arrived, but we are not there yet, although we are certainly well on our way.

Acceptance isn't a mindless act that doesn't require thought and process; far from it. Acceptance involves lots of processing and negotiating various stages that lead us each forward. However, acceptance of one's self, and of the other, in any relationship needs to ask the question: 'What drew us to that person in the first place?' Anyone transitioning from one gender to another would already be 'of that gender' in their thinking, and their behaviour would already mirror many of their desired gender's qualities. If they are in a committed romantic relationship with a partner, they need their partner's commitment to host them throughout the transition process.

It is important to ask the question above because the answer might have been part of the attraction. For example, it's not unlikely the partner was drawn to those masculine or feminine strengths in the first place. As individuals transition to become more of their desired gender, they keep the core of who they are, building a more whole identity around this. When a relationship began, it was the core attraction, including the qualities of the desired gender, which drew the partnership of two people's togetherness, to start with. When Beatrice joined to the core of the person I was, although in every physical way I was a woman, she also was attracted to 'the non-feminine qualities' that existed alongside the womanly. It was not only my apparent gender that drew her. If it was, there would be no way she could accept the male in me. Today, however, she sees the man who has a perceived feminine quality of gentleness to him. This is the core of who I am.

A friend asked if it was easier to transition in today's political and social environment. In many ways it is. It's easier to accept the transition, for both of us, because the current social climate, in our part of Australia, supports acceptance. Beatrice's personality, as an introvert being terrified of exposure, also supports our transition because it's easier being seen as a heterosexual couple than as a homosexual couple. Of course, transitioning is only about one's gender identity and not necessarily about sexual orientation. Many trans guys (from female to male) find themselves drawn to other men and are happier in a homosexual lifestyle. It's not a given that moving into one's gender identity always facilitates opposite sex attraction. I now know that being married to a man was totally 'unnatural' for me because I am heterosexual in my sexual orientation and I am male in my gender identity.

I remember that first session with the psychiatrist in London; I was so exhausted from all the anxiety we had lived with. Beatrice walked with me, hand in hand, through Regent's Park afterwards. The relief and belief we were going to make it was huge. On that day I had no doubt that we would be OK. Of course, there certainly have been days when I haven't felt that way. We might not have made it as a couple if we had been trying to transition 20 years ago.

Clarity

One day in June 2016, after a gruelling morning of intense conversation, a light dawned for Beatrice.

Beatrice: *It's like I lost hope. I was completely taken up by my fears of losing the foundation of who we were in our relationship. I was questioning myself: Maybe I am gay? Maybe I'm not able to adapt to who Wenn is becoming? I had this conflict because I found myself loving Wenn and appreciating the things he did, but it all felt so different. This difference was uncomfortable and I couldn't figure out what it was. I felt so confused. The confusion and discomfort robbed me of feeling good about anything. This became a mountain too difficult to climb over and I found myself catastrophising. Wenn had said he thought the foundation of our relationship, before the transition, had components to it that were unhealthy. Due to the abuses we had each suffered in our childhoods and previous relationships, we tried to make up what we lacked in our own self-esteem, by finding it in each other. The problem with that was that it was shaky ground and depended on the other person 'completing us' all the time. So, when this wasn't forthcoming, the one seeking security, reassurance and self-worth from the other lost ground if we couldn't find it in the other.*

As a woman, Wenn had his male self clothed in a female overcoat, but I had access to the apparent womanhood I saw in Wenn. All that was gentle, patient, long-suffering, slow to anger, emotionally vulnerable, less direct and more likely to notice my needs, the softness and roundness of the female form and all manner of womanly qualities were mine and our relating was dependent upon these. When that overcoat was taken away the very core and foundation of our relationship seemed threatened.

In place of roundness and softness there was squareness and coarseness. Instead of a female voice I heard a male voice. There was no more 'beating about the bush' over decisions that he felt strongly about. If Wenn felt wronged, rather than apologise or go silent for a while, he told me how he was feeling. All of these changes caused me to feel I was losing the love of my life and I sank further and further into loneliness and depression. I was so unhappy with him! How dare he do this to me and how dare he risk our whole relationship to fulfil some whim!

In the past Wenn would smooth out the creases, the faults. When a storm was developing he would blow the clouds away and would always apologise, even when he wasn't at fault. This wasn't only directed towards me; he was like this with everyone. It meant he was often open to abuse. Now, he processes a situation faster and seems much more at home with himself. If someone doesn't like an idea that Wenn has or is a bit distant, rather than Wenn having to work hard to make it up to them or soften them, now he says, 'Whatever!' He is no longer the caretaker for everyone. It's not that he's become an uncaring person, but he is not a doormat any more.

This morning as we talked together I realised, for the first time, that even though Wenn's female overcoat was gone and it was not coming back it was only the outer shell that had gone. Wenn was still here. I realised our relationship was established on much more than simply the female characteristics of who Wenn once was. It was uncomfortable to see Wenn becoming his own person and not always making decisions I agreed with. The grounds for a codependent relationship had shifted and I had been floundering because the once solid rock I thought was beneath us had gone. The reality that hit me though was that this *foundation had so many sandy, unstable and non-trustworthy aspects to it, which were now gone; however, the real essence of who we each were/are, and the true cement that held us, hadn't changed at all!*

For the first time I was able to separate out the abusive male regime I had grown up under from the man Wenn was becoming. I saw Wenn in a different light; one that was not threatening and intimidating but that had been previously prevented from shining due to being buried beneath female clothing. This was still my Wenn. It was the Wenn I loved.

Hope returned to my hurting heart and all I wanted to do was hold him and feel his strong, safe and gentle arms around me.

As Beatrice shared with me what she was discovering I felt humbled and relieved. Like her, I also had a flash of hope for our future. It was heavenly to taste the flavour of connection once again and to discover it hadn't abandoned us. We had lost sight of it in all the pain and grief the transition process had thrown up. Maybe the journey of the past three years was moving us towards resolution – not the resolution I had already experienced since becoming the man I'm meant to be, but the resolution of the difficulty this had brought to our relationship. It was a tenuous thought, but a very real one.

rTMS and ACT

Beatrice: *I found the more I practised 'the essence of ACT and mindfulness', the less the perceived difficulties bothered me. The practice was still new to me and, at times, it was elusive. I think I had stumbled upon an approach to my reactions from the triggers Wenn's maleness prompted. I knew I needed to practise this and not allow my reaction to dominate and dictate my response. It's perfectly fine to feel grief,* *sadness, pain and loss, but it wasn't OK to let these emotions turn into anger and hatred that caused me to abuse the very person I loved most.*

The difficulty was remembering this and recognising the times I was caught away and was failing to separate the issues. At his core, Wenn loved me and valued me. This was not in doubt. He was not my father or my brother or other males from my past who had failed me. He was not abusive, dominant or dictatorial. I simply needed to cement this knowledge so that during the times I couldn't see 'Wenn', only 'male', I was still anchored well enough to enable me to respond and not react.

For us, transitioning wasn't just about gender; it was about our whole identity and personhood. It was about changing our communication style and about choices we needed to make. When two females communicate (even when one of them has a masculinised brain), being socialised as women, they will use female 'tools' to navigate their communication.

In general (of course there are always exceptions), males communicate very differently to females. They may talk with each other side on and often avoid too much eye contact. They may not be as physically demonstrative as women, say the minimum to convey their intention and tend towards plain speaking in direct tones rather than 'beating about the bush'. In general, men are not moody or changeable, are not as emotionally gullible as females and often don't get caught up in gossip and small talk. Men may be more in touch with practical needs and tend to think clearly without having judgements clouded by emotions. These types of changes to my communication style appeared to Beatrice to be happening to me.

Beatrice: *Wenn was now governed, not just by his masculinised brain, but by testosterone coursing through his veins! This hormone was* *responsible for altering Wenn's body so that it resembled the male form and not the female. It was responsible for the hair growth occurring on his body and face. This hormone was responsible for Wenn's muscle development, strength and renewed vitality. It also impacted on Wenn's communication style.*

When it came to cognitively grasping the essence of a situation I saw things clearly and concisely. If Beatrice asked for my opinion, I gave it to her clearly. I didn't go from the question to a perception of what was *really* being asked, nor did I try to think of how to offer an answer so as to least offend or upset. This change in our communication style was very noticeable and Beatrice perceived it as me being less considerate, less emotionally available and less thoughtful. I was simply being the man I had become and didn't see the need to take several steps when one was sufficient! In other words, my response had nothing to do with being less considerate or less sensitive; it was simply focused upon giving the answer that best suited the question. Being 'black and white' and literal, though, wasn't new to us. It was also part of the autistic style to our communication. Many years earlier Beatrice and I had determined we would always be honest with one another, and we wouldn't have it any other way. However, in my previous communication style, I would have softened my comments much more so than I do now.

In many ways our 'literality' contributed to the breakdown of communication between us because we were both inclined this way. Sometimes when speaking with Beatrice I would add 'not literally' so she would know I meant it as a metaphor or a type of description. I was never very good at being metaphorical and tended to say what I meant and to mean what I had said. But this can be viewed as too direct and may cause problems for some females who use more metaphor in their communication style. For example, when asking, 'Hun, I love my new haircut; what do you think?', the person wants the answer that says: 'Yeah, it really suits you.' However, if I think her hair was better before or if I think it needed to be shorter, I'm likely to express this. Some will call it being given to honesty, whilst others will say it's tactless! But essentially there is no malice in my response. I'm not setting out to upset or hurt, I'm simply answering the question from my viewpoint. It's imperative that men and women get to know one another and how they communicate. If this is not a consideration then there will be all sorts of difficulties ahead.

So, as well as acceptance of transition around gender (physical, emotional and mental gender), there needs to be an acceptance also of the changes that accompany these when it comes to expression of who the individual is. This is far deeper and more expansive than 'men are from Mars and women are from Venus', because the changes I was experiencing were unexpected and new. It wasn't like I was born with a male body and my maleness was easily identified. It was much more subtle.

Acceptance is also a choice and not a feeling. For example, at times we learn to accept the weather even when we don't like it, don't want it or don't need it. The changing weather is part of the changing circle of life. It makes me sad when I hear one gender saying negative things about the other. I'm also aware that gender identity may not be so much of a constant as it is a changing state and, for some, being somewhere on the gender spectrum means they 'feel female on some days, male on some and neither on the other days'. Unfortunately most societies have a binary system of gender and there are only two or three 'genders' that are accepted. In Western society it tends to be the two, 'male' or 'female', and nothing outside these or in between! In reality the experience of gender is far wider, just as it is in sexuality. The fluidity of gender is something our society needs to embrace.

I believe once this concept is accepted it will be much kinder for those others transitioning in the future. Currently we grow up with very set ideas about male and female. If a boy favours dolls over guns we are worried! This is a very strange thing. Surely, gentle acceptance of human nature in all of its diversity is so much healthier than trying to fit square pegs into triangular holes!

'Hi Grandpa,' Alicia and Holly (our two older granddaughters) chimed together over the telephone.

'Hi yourselves' came my reply. Giggles echoed down the line, then my daughter was speaking.

'They're very excited,' she said. We loved having 'the girls' come to stay with us, but their Dad had expressed some concern over what they should call me. The girls made the decision for us. 'But Nanna's now a He, so he must be Grandpa.'

I loved the acceptance of these two young children, yet to be spoilt by growing up. However, I'm very happy to be Mum to my own children; I'm just a man-mum, that's all. I don't feel right about them calling me 'Dad' because that's not who I am. I carried them in my womb, nursed them at my breasts and tended to all their needs that required motherly deeds. Being Mum to my children was a gift I would in no way want to cast a shadow over. Those early years were amongst the happiest of my life. Knowing Beatrice also accepted my children and loved them like her own was a bonus.

Us with our granddaughters

For Beatrice and me, being married has also helped in accepting our joint roles as grandparents. Somehow it feels different to when we were in a same sex union. I don't believe it is different though; it's the social concept that has taken root in our psyche and this causes the feeling, the one that says 'this is right'. Of course, this is aided by being in the right gender, finally. Although it's very hard to sort out the social constructed concepts that have dictated our values and morals, I believe that gender identity is not a moral issue; it's a human one.

CHAPTER 12

WHAT WE HAVE LEARNT

Today, it's wet, cold and grey outside. A bit like that winter's day long ago in England when Beatrice and I first met. Our old girl, Star, is asleep on the large, green comfy armchair that used to have a massage setting to it but no longer works. She lies with soft toys lining the chair's arms; it's as if they are looking down upon her as a soft teddy bear might a sleeping child. Just looking at her is relaxing!

'We have all come a very long way,' I say out loud to myself. Our other, younger cat, Queenie, sleeps on her sheepskin upon the large yellow leather, six-seater corner lounge unit, next to me as I type. 'Some things don't change,' I think. 'Family life, with the children growing up; the various cats and dogs that have shared life with us over the years; what a privilege to have known and loved so many different others.'

Mum is now 96 years old. She comes to spend the day with us on Sundays and sits out in the sun room where she can watch the birds in the garden.

On a wintry day like today, she can share a moment with Queenie, watch the glow from the heater, read her novel and enjoy a latte (milky coffee) from her special mug. We give Mum a mug that came from Switzerland originally. It has a black and white cow's head that emerges from the cup base as the drink recedes. The first time we gave her the 'cow mug' she was surprised and laughed. Now, she expects to get that mug each time she visits; it doesn't surprise her any more, it's just familiar and she can count on it.

Mum in the sun room with Queenie

We all need to have familiarity in our lives and those things we can count upon. This includes the people in our lives and what we know about them. When that knowing is challenged and we lose our footing, not only is this scary, it's also difficult to know what to hold onto in its place. For Beatrice and me, we needed to discover that our foundation wasn't being totally withdrawn so much as it was being updated.

Beatrice: *Wenn had always been male and he was never subject to mood swings or the typical contrariness that many of us, as females, live with. Even before the transition Wenn was very 'male' in his thinking, stance and disposition. But because it was hidden from total view in its disguise of the female form, it was less obvious. Also, because Wenn didn't appear to be dictated to by female hormones, as indeed I was/am, he was less 'female' even before the transition. Of course all of this is relative.*

There is a gender spectrum and we all sit at various places along and across this spectrum. Most of us will move seat from time to time and, due to exploration and discovery, will change our minds, change our view, change our fashion likes and so on. This binary world that imposes its concepts of what constitutes male and what constitutes female has much to answer for and, often unwittingly, it contributes to our fears and doubts. We seek certainty and assurance: things we can depend upon. If something presents in a format that is foreign to us and we don't feel prepared for it, we are unsure how to relate to it and often this draws us to criticise and judge.

Then, if we also have bad experiences with an individual, time, place or culture, we are in danger of naming all other associations with that memory and painting them all the same colour. This is what happened to us during the initial stages of Wenn's transition. I lost ground and certainty. All that was familiar fell away and I then associated what was left with my experiences of maleness. Somewhere along the road I lost sight of who Wenn really was and I clothed him with the male overcoat covered from my bad experiences. Each time Wenn was assertive, I saw male dominance. Each time Wenn couldn't be coerced or talked into doing my bidding, I saw male ego and stubbornness. If we look through a window clouded by injured past experience, we will feel the bruises again and fail to see the picture as it is, untainted and pure.

I stand in the kitchen waiting for the kettle to boil so I can make Mum and me a cuppa. Mum is watching the footy on the telly in the lounge room, as she does each Sunday afternoon during the winter football season. I reach up to turn the kettle off as it boils, when rays of warm sunshine pour through the kitchen window alighting upon my head and shoulders. 'Oh lovely,' I say. I haven't felt the warmth of sunshine in a while. I also haven't felt the warmth of Beatrice's embrace in ages, until today. Today, things are different. It isn't that she stopped hugging me or stopped relating to me before today; it is in the quality of that hug. Today there is acceptance and openness. Today there is a touch of welcome and, it seems to me, there is a sense of connection without the fear and hesitation that had dogged her up until today.

Beatrice: *I love you; we have been through an enormous amount of stuff together... It's a bit like those times when we fall out and I hear myself saying, 'That's it, this is the end.' But it isn't. We come to an impasse and it looks like there is no way through, then the clouds move on and the storm passes and I begin to see the sunshine again. When the difficult bit dominates my thinking I don't have access to any other thought. Then I catastrophise that thought and it becomes the worst scenario. I'm learning that this is not the case.*

I'm beginning to understand how my core beliefs influence my thinking. When I experience Wenn being decisive and this leads to a decision Wenn makes that might be different to the one I would make, suddenly it becomes Wenn not thinking of me; I'm not important any more. What's really happening is that Wenn knows what he wants or needs these days and he is not so quick to run it past me. In the past those decisions were made jointly, even the small ones. I now recognise the you in all of this. It's the you I love and the you I want to share the rest of my life with. In the journey of gender discovery we have unearthed not just Wenn's real identity but mine too. It's not simply a heterosexual experience or a homosexual one. It's more to do with seeing beyond the limits of gender and into the core of who we each are and why. Now I get it! It's like the chicken pecking through its prison shell and beginning to get access to the bigger world outside its egg.

Both Beatrice and I have learnt and are still learning so many new, difficult and yet wonderful things that our transitioning together has unearthed. We are thankful our mutual commitment to one another's best has seen us striding together over tumultuous terrain and across chasms we didn't know existed. At times when we wanted to throw in the towel and try an alternative path, each without the other, we hung on in there and didn't run. We still have moments like this and we are constantly challenged to look at our reactions and make choices.

Learning styles

Beatrice and I learn and understand the world very differently; especially when it comes to writing, reading and comprehension of the spoken word. I write poetry, but I seldom go over a poem to re-write it or 'refine' it. It just flows out of me. I'm the same with writing of any kind. With the writing of this, our co-authored book, we nearly came to blows (not literally)! Beatrice needs the structure or scaffolding of approaching something piece by piece. She starts with a skeleton of an idea, which she refines many times, then adds detail, which she also needs to go over and over, and then she will step back and look at the finished product but refine it even further. I 'paint a picture' with words, but rarely look at it again. Once it's finished (in my view) I move onto the next thing. Having to stop and start and revisit so many of the issues described in this text because Beatrice had another thought about some detail, or changed her mind about a feature and wanted it deleted, meant I lost the overall picture and would need to start again! Of course this meant being open again to the same process, as Beatrice needed to further refine that piece of writing!

We have learnt to recognise the core in each other that goes beyond gender into the very depths of who we truly are. Beatrice nourishes my soul and is working hard to know me better. I am trying to resist the feelings of 'injustice' and 'too little too late'. By this I mean I'm working on not taking offence if some of the old core beliefs pop up from time to time for Beatrice and she slips into that dark place of pain and hurt thrust upon her by males who 'should have known better'. We each needed time and space to make adjustments for this new chapter in our lives.

Beatrice: It's interesting, but I wonder if it would have been different if, at the beginning of our relationship, Wenn had been a man? I mean, I know I wished that Wenn had, at that time, but I think that was mostly because of my fear of what others would say rather than because of my initial attraction to him. Although one could argue that I was attracted to the masculine Wenn as well as to the feminine, it was the feminine qualities that drew me the most. I can't imagine being attracted to the masculine Wenn, if that had been more dominant. So, what would it mean if somehow it had been the feminine Wenn (housed within the male) that was ultimately the gender he was more at home with and this would have meant transitioning from male to female? Would things have ultimately worked out this well for us? I guess I think this echoes the reality, that even though Wenn is male the female draws my attention first, and it's only because I know the fuller Wenn that I can still relate to and love you – the Wenn you are now.

This is a daunting thought and one I don't have an answer for. I can only comment on what our experience has been and not what might have been if I had been a male to female trans person. It is an interesting question though!

Beatrice: *When we were first drawn to each other I was very young. The timing for Wenn's transition some 32 years later takes into account our long-standing relationship and commitment to each other. I would not have been able to accept Wenn as a guy back then, especially since so much of the baggage we have dealt with now was very much present in my life, but at a subconscious level. I wouldn't have been ready to look at all of that then. I remember when I first was upset that Wenn was not male and he said: 'I'll be Will for you and change into the man you need me to be.' I was horrified at the thought.*

But as we have moved on in our lives, although this has totally changed and I recognise the truth of who Wenn is, I also was very content with how our lives were. Of course, I understand that I have been able to deal with such a lot of emotional baggage from the early childhood hurts that wouldn't have been noticed, let alone dealt with, had our journey not necessitated it.

We are both so much more whole as individuals these days, even though this is still a work in progress.

As far as attraction goes, I only know I am very definitely attracted to the female. If the shoe had been on the other foot I'm not sure I could have done what Beatrice has done. I am very much drawn to the female her, and in my sexual orientation, only attracted to the female. I cannot imagine being attracted to the male. Having said this though, Beatrice has aspects to her that could be interpreted as masculine. She is a strong woman, has broad shoulders and a slightly masculine style in her walk, reasoning and practical strength; her mum always said Beatrice took after her dad! She loves to chop wood for the fire, fix things that are broken and usually keeps her emotions to herself. She is not a social bug and avoids gossip. But she is gentle and has those feminine qualities of compassion, softness and of being very changeable! Perhaps this is more about who she is though than women in general; maybe I'm doing that thing of stereotyping and lumping the genders together rather than appreciating the wider gender spectrum. Old habits die hard!

Where does this take us? I think we need to acknowledge the grief and loss the other will feel from time to time. The gains I have accessed and which are allowing me to thrive have caused grief for Beatrice, but as she sorts through her losses and comes to terms with them we will be free to enjoy the gains and further joint adventures together.

It takes time and energy to build a new identity, but it can only start as we learn to let go of the old one. It's not a matter of the older one being better; it's more to do with its familiarity and comfort. Setting up home in a new country where they speak a different language, have different currency and different times for different things is very unsettling, to say the least. I know we can do this. I know because I trust in the love that drew us together originally and has held us together over the past 32 years.

Some might argue that it's habit and routine that kept us under the same roof. I know that it's far deeper than this. If it was only habit (better the devil you know) we would not have survived the journey to date. Habit doesn't have deep enough roots unless it is tinted with love and commitment. The roots of our love go beyond the gender barrier and run deep beyond the chasms and cliffs that rise up to meet us. As we learn to forgive those things we can't change and challenge those we can, we will see flowers growing in wasteland allowing butterflies to alight and feed.

I am confident that for us this struggle will be worthwhile and it will make us stronger and wiser human beings. I know that not all couples will survive one of them changing their gender, and it's important to be honest with oneself. There is no defeat in owning one's own reality, and none of us has the right to judge the other. We are all individuals and face battles with history that are not so easy to recover from. Some soldiers get up and return to the battlefield; others need to go home. There is no shame in this, it is what it is!

I have been fortunate to have Beatrice by my side each step of the way. Sometimes we were not in tune with each other and sometimes we were out of step, but we kept going forward. Neither of us knew what the future held, but neither of us was willing to turn back the clock either. When I asked Beatrice if she would want me to return to the woman I once was and lose my male overcoat, she emphatically stated: 'No.'

It begs the question, at least for us, whether my transition was ever only about my gender or if uniting the Wenn with all the right bits of himself was much deeper than this, for both of us. Could it be that the whole process of 'change' was more influential upon our joint transition than we had realised? There are still many unanswered questions, but currently this journey continues and we anticipate it opening more doors as we go on.

One of the hardest things was letting the past lie, knowing it to be firmly part of who we each are and trusting that it's done its job in our hearts and lives. This allows and contributes to a firm foundation from which to spring to other, yet unknown, places that are ahead of us. We travel holding our heads high and in the knowledge that we are loved. For us, this is the bottom line. Having each other's acceptance, love and welcome means more to each of us than anything else.

Would I do this all again? Yes, I would. At times it's hard coming to terms with the reality that I missed a timely puberty where becoming a man was a process that other boys were sharing in, together. I'll never have the experience of being born and brought up as a boy. I'll only have the memories that fuelled the feelings of wishing I had been. But I'm one of the fortunate ones. I've been not only able to realise my lack of wholeness and the disparities in my gender, I've been able to do something about it. I've been able to transition fully into the man I truly am.

For some, transition will be adopting the identity and desired gender of who they've come to know is truly them, but without any other intervention. They are so because they say so! But for others there will be a strong and compulsive need to transition using hormones to alter their appearance. Then for others, such as myself, there will be a strong desire for surgical intervention too. If individuals have to do this on their own, without the love, acceptance and support of their family and friends, I cannot imagine the isolation and pain it would cause. Human beings are designed for community, even though the level of human interaction is different for each of us. We are not designed to go it alone! In the trans world the suicide rate is as high as 40 per cent.[1]

Having the acceptance I have had from my friends and family enabled me to explore this aspect of my life. When I went to tell the children and I asked Katy to sit down because I had something to tell her, she said, 'You're having a sex change, aren't you?' I asked her why this came to mind and not something else, like maybe I had some terrible ailment or was going to separate from my beloved!

She said, 'It's always been on the cards Mum...we have known this about you for ages! But I'm not going to start calling you Dad; I don't need another one of those!'

'I know, my sentiments exactly,' I said. 'I'm a man-mum!'

I'm fortunate that my sons accept my transitioning too, and I'm sure it's not so easy for them. When Mother's Day came around this year the children wondered how to acknowledge Beatrice and me. Katy said, 'I wanted to get you a card, Mum, but they were all too girly!' Maybe there's a market out there for a wider array of cards that are not so gender specific. I know it's now much easier to buy a card for 'partner' or sweetheart these days, and not only wife or husband. I was delighted when this began to be the norm, and look forward to an even wider variety of cards that encompasses our ever-changing society.

Words for life

The surgeon I recently consulted to perform reparative surgery upon me said, 'It's not sex reassignment surgery; it's sex assignment!' He told me also that I would do well to move

---

1   See http://thinkprogress.org/lgbt/2015/06/22/3672506/transgender-suicide-rates and www.vocativ.com/culture/lgbt/transgender-suicide

beyond the label of 'trans man' to simply being 'a man'. He said that acceptance of the full person I was meant leaving 'transition' behind and moving on into the man I now was; if I only thought of myself as a 'trans man' I might never truly or fully own my male identity. But I think transitioning and moving on in one's life is an ongoing journey that we all can take. There is always some new thing to learn or to unlearn!

Although I understand his intention to affirm my male gender, I think for some, being trans is an identity all on its own. To arrive at the understanding I am trans is to arrive at the understanding that my gender identity is across from the cis gender I was assigned at birth; I am not female, but I am male. Being a trans man is saying I am male, but it's not how my journey was viewed in the beginning. If I fail to own or recognise the trans aspect to me, I am in denial of the journey I have been on.

I was afraid of adopting the male identity because this wasn't the body I was born with. Moving beyond my cis gender and using 'trans' terminology is actually an accurate description of who I am. It could fog up the window and cloud the picture of the man I have grown more fully into, but only if I let it. The doctor said to me: 'You are as much a man as I am or any other man is. It's difficult that you started out housed in the wrong body, but your journey just took you places most of us miss out on and you had a few more countries to visit before you finally came home.' So, you see, I have come to understand I am a man with a trans history! To him and his team I shall always be grateful!

Now Beatrice and I are continuing to learn how to practise being home. I'm not used to staying in one place and I like to keep a bag packed, just so I'm keeping my options open! It's OK to have a bag on standby; it's all part of the process. It's not that I dislike being where I am or that I'm unhappy; it's more about the gypsy in me. I'm at home in so many different spaces, and part of feeling at home is connected to moving around to touch base with other places; it's the way I am. I'm also conscious that being on the move was connected to being on the run. My family tended to move around a lot, which prevented us from out-staying our welcome in any one place. A part of me still feels this way today. If we don't put roots down we don't need to fear being uprooted!

I hadn't recognised this was also part of the ideology that prevented me from transitioning earlier on in my life. This morning, over our morning cuppa in bed, Beatrice said:

I think what I realise is that the sexes are not really that far apart. Maybe because we have both transitioned in our understanding (you are now physically male and not just a butch lesbian), I can see that you are still you. We are very different people, but your difference isn't this big 'macho male' thing that I'd always thought of about men, like men being on the other side, over there somewhere; bullies, dominant, patriarchal and in control of everything. This is still the case at times, but this isn't you. I carry around this old cliché that all men are like this, even though I've known intellectually this is not the case. It's only more of a reality since your transition.

I've misread you! Your deeper voice, your decisiveness and confidence of what it represents have threatened my sense of self. I'm learning to challenge my thinking and appreciate that's not you. I'm learning to welcome the male in you, just as I did the female, rather than reject who you are.

At first it felt like you had changed 'sides' and you were now 'one of them'! I felt very uncomfortable with all you represented. It just isn't like that any more. I can see the male you but I also see your softness, your care and the core of who you are, which hasn't changed. It's one thing to work through the negatives of my experience of men but it's another to go beyond that and be able to grow into acceptance of the male you.

In doing this I'm finding I'm more accepting in general of men in the outside world. I'm seeing people and the person, rather than my perception of their gender.

Her words and our discussions have opened so many connections for us. I am increasingly aware of the wider implications, especially because we are also autistic. One psychologist told Beatrice she didn't think she was autistic, because she had 'good eye contact'. Autism is so much bigger than that. Many females on the spectrum are not being taken seriously as girls and women on the spectrum because they don't 'appear' to have the disabling features seen in so many spectrum males. It's vital we change our thinking on this and see past the apparent obvious. Outward behaviour can be modelled, learnt and modified. It's not always giving the accurate picture of an individual's inner life and experience. Secretly, I was 'Will' in my deepest being. Just because Will wasn't apparent to others did not negate his presence. Then, in years to come when Will felt stronger and more sure of his existence, he was uncaged and allowed to roam free. Some have said that since this event has occurred in Wenn, autism isn't so obvious in him. But, what they are seeing in Wenn's autism could be characteristics that blend in more with being thought of as traditionally 'male'; for example, less typically female indecisiveness compared to being more decisive, more at home and more confident than ever before. The areas I still wrestle with haven't gone away so much as they have changed direction somewhat and, at times, are less troublesome due to having more courage to give it a go!

That place of living with a more male-disposed brain but having female hormones coursing through my body placed me at a disadvantage! I constantly experienced this battle of being drawn one way while travelling through a fog that hindered my view and prevented me from seeing clearly. One of the differences transition has made, due to uniting these aspects of who I am, is in giving me the clarity to see and comprehend the factors involved with decision making. Some research is saying autism and gender dysphoria tend to occur together more often than gender dysphoria within the neurotypical population. From my perspective this may be so. But other research that is suggesting treating gender dysphoria is a cure for autism may be failing to comprehend this division of the person's psyche.

Due to the dysphoria, many other dislocations were occurring with my ability to process and understand social mores. Although the dysphoria, once lessened, enabled more connections due to having the appropriate hormones leading the charge, this didn't change my difficulties with processing social situations or of making language more available to me. I hope researchers of these topics will consider the wider issues of autism when looking at the evidence of the varying changes occurring, once gender dysphoria is less invasive of a person's experience.

Beatrice: From transitioning with Wenn, becoming more aware of the fuller essence of male, listening to the radio and watching men in various roles, I've become more aware of them as human beings and individuals rather than sharing the collective, black and white, outdated belief that men are the stereotypical, insensitive half of the human race whereas women are the caring and sensitive half. The transition process has forced me to look at my core beliefs and challenge these. Otherwise we wouldn't have survived this process and we couldn't be together.

Wenn's transition process was to join his body and mind to being one in his masculinity; mine was to transition from being fearful, angry and hostile towards maleness and more open to seeing the value in who and what being male can offer. It's also been about overcoming my inability to relate intimately to a man, due to past hurts, and it is enabling me to accept myself, becoming more independently the adult woman and not so much the pouting child.

At the beginning of this process I said to Wenn I couldn't imagine loving a man. I wondered if it would mean, if we stayed together, sleeping in separate rooms! What I've come to understand is Wenn is still Wenn; I love him. Maybe my sexual attraction is more fluid than I had realised. I still miss aspects of Wenn that no longer exist. I still grieve the loss of the 'woman', but in reality we have put people into boxes to make sense of them when the box has simply enabled us to structure a response. It's just not that black and white! It's all still uncomfortable and I don't like it. The big difference now, even though it still hurts, is that I can separate the issues of my past experiences and beliefs about 'men and male' to what is Wenn being the man he is.

Her empathy towards me and her feelings of wanting me to explore my masculinity meant she encouraged me to grow a beard...such a different place from where she had been once. When I first told her of my desire to explore transitioning from female to male, her words were those of shock and alarm: 'But you won't grow a beard or anything, will you?'

Beatrice: I'm becoming more and more aware that I have to learn how to relate to men. I'm building more of an awareness of the 'commonality' that men share which I'd not given attention to before. I shut men out of my life unless I needed to relate to them.

Beatrice stroking my beard!

We've always had some lovely male friends in our lives, but I never recognised them as 'male' in the sense of my belief system; somehow the male issue didn't present. But I didn't incorporate the understanding that men can be gentle, sensitive and loving into my psyche at that time either. Our transitioning together has enabled me to join the dots better and see beyond the stereotype.

I'd not realised I had been carrying around some awfully rancid, toxic waste that was causing me to sour my relationships where males were concerned. This journey has exposed that baggage and I've chosen to dispose of it. Instead I view this new territory as a type of compost to grow good things between us, even though it will take time and practice. This new era is one I'm learning to welcome and choose to see the positive rather than the negative. I know it's not easy and, at times, I'm unsure how to 'be' around the Wenn he now is, but it will unfold and it will improve. We are in uncharted waters and we need to give ourselves time and space to rediscover what it means for us.

This morning I noticed a new wind was blowing over us. I felt such a strong connection to Beatrice and couldn't hold her close enough!

Beatrice: *It was reassuring to feel sexually inclined towards Wenn again. I was sitting in my chair looking at him as he interacted with a guest who was visiting for morning tea. I felt such a love and a drawing towards him...it almost feels like we have moved on from the pain and angst I felt before. We have reached a point where our relationship is moving into a different chapter, certainly one much more settled.*

We had moved from the point where we felt and experienced a crash, a disconnection, much like I imagine a couple might feel going through a divorce. I had lost hope that we would ever connect again as we once had. Now, I know for certain that we are and will always be each other's best friend. I have my Wenn, and life couldn't be fuller!